Ludwig van Beethoven, String quartet Opus 132, Third movement: *"Heiliger Dankgesang eines Genesenen an die Gottheit, in der lydischen Tonart"* (Holy song of thanksgiving of a convalescent to the Deity, in the Lydian Mode).

Human Development, Language and the Future of Mankind

The Madness of Culture

Louis S. Berger

Consultant and Independent Practitioner
Formerly based at Southwest Research Institute and University
of Louisville School of Medicine

First published 2014 by
PALGRAVE MACMILLAN

Palgrave Macmillan in the UK is an imprint of Macmillan Publishers Limited, registered in England, company number 785998, of Houndmills, Basingstoke, Hampshire RG21 6XS.

Palgrave Macmillan in the US is a division of St Martin's Press LLC, 175 Fifth Avenue, New York, NY 10010.

Palgrave Macmillan is the global academic imprint of the above companies and has companies and representatives throughout the world.

Palgrave® and Macmillan® are registered trademarks in the United States, the United Kingdom, Europe and other countries.

ISBN 978–1–137–41526–4

This book is printed on paper suitable for recycling and made from fully managed and sustained forest sources. Logging, pulping and manufacturing processes are expected to conform to the environmental regulations of the country of origin.

A catalogue record for this book is available from the British Library.

Library of Congress Cataloging-in-Publication Data
Berger, Louis S.
   Human development, language, and the future of mankind : the madness of culture / Louis S. Berger, Independent Practitioner, USA.
      pages   cm
   ISBN 978–1–137–41526–4
   1. Psychology—Philosophy.   2. Human behavior—Philosophy.
   3. Psycholinguistics—Philosophy.   4. Civilization—Philosophy.
   5. Social problems—Philosophy.   I. Title.
   BF38.B457 2014
   150—dc23   2014018845

Transferred to Digital Printing in 2014

To Louie,
With your love and guidance, you saved me. With this book,
your final work, you can help save mankind; hopefully
mankind will listen and learn.
Eternally grateful,
Your wife,
Andrea

Contents

1
Understanding Our Global Dangers

Questions that need to be asked

Nobody likes to think about it, but it is undeniable that humanity is facing grave threats. Especially dangerous are the 'two problems for our species' survival – nuclear war, and environmental catastrophe'.[1] It is neither obvious nor certain that the human species can survive.[2]

Humankind has created these perils, and more – poverty, disease, famine, genocide, hatred and overpopulation. How could that have happened in the first place? How could we have allowed ourselves to drift into these awful conditions? How could we stand idly by and watch them arise, evolve and assume such enormous proportions? But perhaps even more to the point, now that we are facing these dangerous situations, how is it that although we did create them, we are unable to reverse them? It isn't because we haven't tried. Some perils, war for instance, have been with us for a very long time (although in much tamer forms until Hiroshima and Nagasaki), while others, such as the environmental crises, are comparatively recent, but there have been numerous and continual efforts, some longstanding, to head off these and others. Doesn't the fact that while we are responsible for our dire circumstances we apparently cannot ameliorate them, call for an explanation? Why the continual failures? Why does it now even seem that these threats are alien, not of our own making, to be coming from some unknown, otherworldly external forces beyond our control? (For instance, we now have 'the threat of nuclear war', a depersonalized, looming ogre. Where are the war-makers? It is getting more and more difficult to remain aware that these dangers have human origins.) What are we missing, what accounts for humankind's apparent inability to

1

control its own destiny? What would it take to undo these dangers that we ourselves have created?

These, broadly, are the questions that this book raises and addresses. It joins countless past and present analyses and explanations of the world's ills undertaken from a variety perspectives and disciplines. It is safe to say that not only have these analyses, explanations and suggestions failed to lead to any substantial improvement in our lot, but that in spite of them the world's overall situation continues to deteriorate greatly.[3] There is ample ground, then, for viewing yet another restorative attempt and proposal such as this one with skepticism and suspicion. Why should it fare any better than the multitude of its predecessors?

Certainly the odds against bringing about change are great, but I suggest that the enterprise isn't entirely hopeless. There is room for cautious optimism because, as I see it, there are several important differences between this and the preceding efforts. For one thing, the goal of most extant works is to propose strategies for countering the threats. Here, the prime focus will be on understanding why standard kinds of strategy have invariably failed. But a more significant difference is in the underlying framework. Although they appear to come from a variety of positions and disciplines, actually the attempts share a certain tacit foundation – a master framework as it were. I believe that it is the undesirable features of that covert base that account for the failures of the varied remedial approaches.

The ground of the present work differs drastically from that common foundation. It is unorthodox, incorporating certain unconventional models of human development, ontogenetic as well as phylogenetic, that are ignored in other attempts, and I believe it is the inclusion of these developmental considerations that gives this effort a better chance of success. That is, by looking carefully at certain key developmental events, this effort is able to offer otherwise unavailable insights – more fundamental, penetrating and useful ways of understanding the nature of our global threats and of the reasons for past failures. Therefore, it may be able to lead to original, better approaches to our dilemmas, to envision remedial approaches that now are precluded by our flawed perspectives. That is the reason for my cautious optimism.

A history of failed remedial efforts

To start, let us take a look at some representative examples of the long parade of previous remedial efforts to improve the world's lot. These have come from a range of disciplines, including biology, neuropsychobiology, engineering, physics, systems analysis, psychology, medicine, the mental health professions, sociology, law, economics, political science, history, anthropology, sociobiology, philosophy and religion. A range of analyses has resulted in a variety of proposals to explain the nature and origins of our difficulties and to recommend the remedies that follow. For example, one common position is that our problems stem from humankind's innate destructiveness, an appealingly simple, reductionist explanation that supports fatalism and persists in the face of a considerable amount of contradictory scientific evidence.[4] These days, perhaps the most common orientation of analyses and corrective recommendations is scientific and technological. It is almost de rigeur to presuppose that regardless of their origins, our difficulties can and must be dealt with by cutting-edge science and technology.[5]

Another common approach is illustrated in efforts to eliminate warfare. The exchanges that took place in the early 1930s between Albert Einstein and Sigmund Freud may be dated but they still are prototypical and instructive. Einstein was not exactly a fan of psychology. In a diary entry about the important Swiss psychiatrist Carl Jung, he wrote:

> I understand Jung's vague, unprecise notions, but I consider them worthless: a lot of talk without any clear direction. If there has to be a psychiatrist, I should prefer Freud. I do not believe in him, but I love very much his concise style and his original, although rather extravagant, mind.[6]

Einstein's objections to psychiatry and psychoanalysis were those that one might expect from a natural scientist, even from a creative one. He objected to logically weak, inadequately empirically supported theorizing, and so his disapproval of Freud's work was based mostly on psychoanalysis's failure to live up to science's standards of rigor, internal consistency, empirical confirmation, quantification and the like. In general, his writings indicate that although in important ways he was a humanist, Einstein was not what clinicians call 'psychologically minded'. His thought, even though revolutionary, was still formalistic, mathematical, abstract, lofty, objective and depersonalized. Freud sensed this. Although he had no doubts about the significance of Einstein's work as a physicist, apparently he didn't think much of the latter's psychological understanding. In a letter to a friend, Freud wrote: 'Several years ago I had a long talk with him [Einstein] during which I realized, to my amusement, that he knows no more about psychology than I do about mathematics.'[7] Einstein later modified his criticism of Freud and even 'approached Freud in his [Einstein's] attempt to assemble a group of intellectual leaders and, subsequently, suggested that Freud engage him in a public discussion about how mankind could be delivered from the menace of war'.[8]

The discussions took place in 1939. Under the auspices of the International Institute of Intellectual Co-operation, Einstein invited Freud to publicly exchange thoughts about the causes of and cure for wars. Einstein became convinced that recent efforts to prevent war had failed because 'strong psychological factors are at work which paralyze these efforts'.[9] In retrospect, what these exchanges illustrate is that, together, the best that even this pair of intellectual giants could come up with were mostly standard, familiar analyses and proposals, except for a few ideas and concepts that were imported by Freud from the then generally unfamiliar field of psychoanalysis. The two formulated the problematic issues and conceptualized remedial rationales and actions mostly in the usual social, political and military contexts. They saw the causes of war primarily in standard terms, such as the availability of weaponry and the refusal to disarm; conflicting political motives of nations; the craving for power of the governing class, which among other consequences stimulates collective psychosis; conflicts between individuals and small groups; malignant forms of government; the erotic and aggressive instincts shared by humans and other animals;[10] and self-centered nationalism. Other than for some of the recommendations that reflected psychoanalytic thought,[11] the solutions that followed were also mostly the familiar traditional ones: to disarm; establish a world government and a world court with executive force; establish and consult with an international group of eminent intellectuals; elect better leaders; restructure the form of society (socialism is the system preferred by both); or to enlist the support of religious groups.

Neither Freud nor Einstein were naive about the chances of controlling aggression in individuals or in nations. Freud, especially, emphasized the recalcitrance, the obstinateness, of human aggressive destructiveness.[12] Their exchanges are marked by an undertone of bleak pessimism. It is especially worth noting that, in an aside, Freud made an unusual, almost radical observation that is very much in line with one of the key theses of this book. He noted that 'cultural progress' not only can improve civilization's conditions but also 'may well lead to the extinction of mankind'[13] – as I see it, an insightful, perceptive, highly unconventional observation that still goes against consensual, uncritically accepted rosy views of 'cultural progress'. His thought should to have been taken more seriously by his peers and contemporaries, and should be taken more seriously by us. A developmentally focused version of this position will be developed in the later chapters.

All this of course took place well before anyone could foresee the development of today's weapons of mass destruction. More than a decade later, shortly after the destruction of Hiroshima and Nagasaki, Einstein made the much-quoted statement that

> The unleashed power of the atom has changed everything save our modes of thinking and we thus drift toward unparalleled catastrophe... A new type of thinking is essential if mankind is to survive and move toward higher levels... Today we must abandon competition and secure co-operation... Past thinking methods did not prevent world wars [but] future thinking *must* prevent wars... Our defense is not in armaments, nor in science, nor in going underground.[14]

Some 50 years after, that the psychoanalyst Hanna Segal stated:

> We have not come to realize that the advent of the atomic weapons made meaningless the idea of a just war, or the defense of civilized values, since the war would destroy all values... I am afraid that the atomic bomb may have changed our thinking for the worse.[15]

So much for the effectiveness of almost a century of analyses of our ills and the associated solutions, and for the impact of reality. (Reality is a notoriously difficult, slippery, controversial subject, and will be central to the argument that I will unfold. I postpone a more extended consideration until Chapter 6, because that calls for a good deal of preparatory work. Until then, I will often use the term casually, flexibly or intuitively.)

It is all too evident now that although there have apparently been notable advances in psychology, psychiatry, psychoanalysis, political science, history, anthropology, the natural sciences and technology, which have supposedly advanced our understanding of war's causes, still our conceptions of available remedies, of what we see as available options for countering the threats, haven't changed fundamentally. Increasing our armaments, remaining competitive and superior, using threats and intimidation, attempting to negotiate, use bribery, form coalitions, hold peace conferences and the like remain our sole and standard means of trying to intervene. All of these are variants of an effort to change the adversary's mind and practices – as we will see, not necessarily the only option. At any rate, the nefarious symptoms of seething conflict remain. We are still plagued by racism, extremes of poverty and wealth, fanatical and hostile nationalism, genocide, oppression of women, egocentric and exploitive acts that destroy the environment, lack of education, lack of communication, loss of spirituality, growing arsenals of unimaginably destructive weapons, gross economic inequality and religious hatred, and these conditions are still blamed for the threats' persistence and the chronic violence. Worse, the world is almost never free of highly destructive warfare going on somewhere.

Current attempts are still drawing on the old familiar spectrum of remedial approaches, although perhaps implemented with some new technological wrinkles. Our situation has failed to improve since the era of the Einstein–Freud exchanges. Not only is it also painfully obvious that the have threats persisted but, because of our continuing scientific-technological 'advances', the nature and scope of these threats have become ever more destructive.

Let us ask what conceptual frameworks and what worldviews have grounded this large collection of investigations and remedial efforts? There is no obvious answer, and that in itself is telling. I haven't seen this question even raised. Thus much if not all of the corpus of extant remedial approaches floats on air. Whatever their foundations may be, they remain unspecified and implicit. It seems that the experts just wade in, oblivious of and indifferent to their presuppositions, and start analyzing and making recommendations without examining their groundwork, the vast body of assumptions on which the arguments rest. The results are predictable. Unexamined conceptual foundations typically lead to unexamined, poorly grounded solutions. My constant refrain is going to be that the nature of the conceptual underpinnings of these remedial efforts does need our most careful attention. Unearthing that ground will reveal flaws that have played a key role in the failed attempts. Indeed, one of the basic premises of this work, one that will be restated in various aspects throughout this work is that a radically new perspective or worldview (meaning the combined view of self, world and language) is needed if we want to become able to conceptualize effective solutions.

The shortcomings of symptom removal

I claimed that history tells us that none of the identified approaches has worked, but that is true only to a limited extent. There have been, and continue to be, pockets of progress – for example, our gains in civil rights. The trouble is that when one looks at these isolated gains carefully, it becomes evident that (at least) in most cases they have had relatively little staying power. Benign gains are temporary and are lost. The usual pattern is that regressive forces reassert themselves and regain lost ground. Why is that? A pattern that repeats in various guises is that first, after much struggle, reformers have managed to achieve their goals. The majority have imposed their benign, beneficial reform views 'democratically', typically through sanctioned political action. However, that amounts to socially approved coercion, and history tells us that in most cases the progress achieved by such well-intentioned, legally sanctioned, one-sided actions brings only temporary relief. Sooner or later (and usually sooner) the old noxious patterns and opponents reassert themselves with a vengeance. That is because the nefarious, regressive needs and wishes of the powerful minority forces have not been dealt with adequately, if at all. In essence, the 'cure' of the social ill had been cosmetic. It did not attend to the dynamics underlying the conflict between the opposing forces. The underlying ills had not been resolved but had only gone underground. Historically, self-centered groups have been more focused, single-minded and persistent than the reformers, and all too often more successful. The unrelenting, tenacious forces bide their time, and at an opportune moment they reassert themselves successfully, and the cycle starts all over again. Currently there is no shortage of examples illustrating just this phenomenon.

What happens in these cases is analogous to an all too familiar pattern in the therapy of individuals. It is what therapists call a cure through 'symptom removal'. A superficial 'therapy' fails to attend properly to the underlying destructive dynamics, concentrating instead on the tangible phenomena that were only the symptoms – and poorly understood symptoms at that. The achieved results were unstable. In this model we can say that even when they have been successful to some degree, past efforts to resolve the world's problems have failed to recognize, let alone take into consideration, the world's underlying pathology, its madness. We need to make sure that any amelioration of the world threats that we achieve is not such a cosmetic solution. Such a symptom-removing cure may very well turn out to be worse than the disease. So, we need to make sure first that we understand what is wrong with the way we have been looking at our severe difficulties, that we understand our pathology – and that calls for an examination of the current framework and also for developing genuinely different one that will provide an adequate grasp for future use. It may not be readily apparent, but if we aren't very careful, relying primarily on science and technology to solve our difficulties – say, global warming – may be such a questionable, potentially destructive cosmetic 'cure'. The issue here is, are science and technology really neutral, equally capable of good as well as evil? This question of science's neutrality will be considered in chapter 6. As E. F. Schumacher tells us,

> [w]hen the level of the knower is not adequate to the level (or grade of significance) of the object of knowledge, the result is not factual error but something much more serious: an inadequate and impoverished view of reality.[16]

'Selfish' behaviors

Let us look more closely at one of the standard explanations offered for the intractability of our difficulties – namely, the destructive, obstructionistic, selfish behaviors of powerful egocentric individuals such as corporation executives and key politicians, of political organizations or of entire nations. Blind, callous egocentrism is just human nature, we are told. Let us ask an apparently strange question: Are these kinds of destructive behavior usually really selfish or greedy? Are they really in the blackguards' best interests? For example, a politician who for his own gain blocks legislation aimed at putting appropriate environmental or financial controls in place, or a corporation that is polluting or raping the environment, or a nation that is accumulating more and better weapons of mass destruction – are all of these entities really acting selfishly? The obvious answer is yes, of course. All such acts are patently self-serving, callously indifferent to the welfare of others and provide benefits to the wrongdoers. We are sure that these opponents stand in the way of enacting known desirable solutions such as those proposed in the Einstein–Freud exchanges. Isn't it obvious that these nefarious forces impede actions or strategies that much of humanity sees as obviously humane for their own benefit?

That is the consensus, and it seems folly to question it. However, on further reflection, that belief seems less credible. One can see that there is more to this kind of supposed selfishness than meets the eye. If one looks more carefully, it isn't all that difficult to see that in very many, if not in most, such cases, the supposed antisocial, egocentric behaviors really aren't selfish at all: in the long run they are obviously self-destructive, and so they are the very antithesis of truly selfish acts. About the only way one can make sense of the disastrous path on which corporations, governments, and the super-rich are taking the world is if they believe that they can survive a nuclear holocaust. There are rumors that this is a growing belief, strategy and practice.[17] In most cases, these kinds of act abet the mass destruction of the globe, and that is going to benefit no one – not even the villains. Our hypothetical 'selfish' polluting corporation is going to have a difficult time making money if and when 'it' has no more customers, staff, executives, stock holders and stock brokers, no banks available, when all of the other collateral resources on which it necessarily relies (energy sources, food and water, breathable air, experts of various kind) are gone. The entity simply will not be able to continue to exist – and everyone knows that, or should know that. The same holds for the nation arming itself to the teeth with weapons of mass destruction. Isn't it obvious? If the globe is destroyed, corporations, nations, selfish individuals will be destroyed along with everyone and everything else. From this perspective it ought to be glaringly apparent that in many situations what we commonly and unquestioningly regard as selfish acts that need to be combated by well-intentioned people actually are not selfish at all. They are self-destructive. The offending entity does not see that, or does not believe that its time would come, or doesn't care – or it is mad (in a sense to be developed later), believing that its survival can be assured. Similar considerations apply to the apparently selfish behavior of ordinary individuals acting 'selfishly' in minor ways, such as needlessly, thoughtlessly and self-indulgently wasting resources.

These behaviors are puzzling and paradoxical, and they call for better understanding. They make little sense, although they can be made to seem understandable: they can be explained away simplistically by hand-waving – for example, by invoking some supposed (scientifically validated?) innate destructive or selfish urges. The situation can't be that simple. Take corporate behavior, for example. Few corporations are run by dunces. Usually, executives and other major decision-makers are well educated, successful, worldly, experienced and analytical, although they certainly may be amoral, even profoundly immoral, antisocial or even psychopathic. In any case, in making their decisions they must take many complex variables into consideration, perform complex analyses, make forecasts based on sophisticated reasoning (often on esoteric complex mathematical models). They have considerable resources available. They are likely to have had some successes since they have survived in a competitive world. All of this makes their selfishness difficult to understand, given that the ultimate destruction to which they are contributing is not difficult to see. Why do such persons fail to recognize and act in their actual best interests? Why aren't they truly egocentric and don't they act really selfishly to assure their survival? Why is it that they persist in, say, thinking in terms of the short-term bottom-line profit, thereby making their own demise more than likely? It is understandable that they may want to satisfy some short-term goals. Not easily understood is why they fail to realize that what they are doing harms not only others whom they may not care about but ultimately also themselves and their loved ones. Doesn't this strange situation merit more careful consideration? (The weaknesses of explaining such acts as manifestations of innate human nature will be considered later.) Do not the self-destructive choices by presumably competent people and groups need a better explanation? Do we have a satisfactory answer?

The context can be enlarged. One can similarly ask why it is that nations persist in following 'selfish' paths that will almost certainly lead to their own destruction. Why aren't nations really, realistically, self-centered? What is the explanation? As will become evident in the later chapters, I see that kind of paradoxical behavior as symptomatic and prototypical of our central difficulties. At any rate, it seems strange, but in our culture such paradoxical behaviors remain largely unrecognized and unaddressed. We are sure that we already know why people and entities act in destructive ways, and we shrug our shoulders. We have ready and mostly uncontested explanations. So it is seldom recognized or discussed that these 'selfish' acts aren't really selfish and are thus highly paradoxical. We just see nefarious people, corporations or nations – opponents, enemies and villains whose behaviors have to be blocked, who have to be defeated. (Our behavior, of course, is not self-destructive.) And so we improve our armaments.

At any rate, these kinds of common explanation for egocentrisms are not only superficial and inadequate but come close to embodying *virtus dormitiva* fallacies. All too often they rely on circular reasoning: we have warfare because human nature is aggressive, war-like; we have selfish behaviors because humans are selfish; we are greedy because people want to accumulate things; people go into competition because they want to be the best; we overeat because we are gluttonous; we fail to exercise because we are lazy; and so on. More sophisticated explanations will draw on various disciplines for support (genetic research does show that there is a selfish gene), but their reasoning is not much better, although the circularities are better disguised.

Symptoms of madness

I believe that this class of baffling, paradoxical selfish/self-destructive behaviors can tell us something important about the roots of our problems. Over the years of doing individual psychotherapy and related clinical work in a variety of settings, I, like most therapists, have encountered a good deal of self-destructive behavior, often in the guise of the kinds of apparently self-centered, gratifying action and belief mentioned above. In the therapeutic setting it is relatively easy to recognize and understand disguised self-destructive behaviors and beliefs as symptoms of individuals' pathology. Little by little, it has dawned on me that the same pattern is pervasive in our culture as a whole and that it inescapably points to, and is one of the ubiquitous symptoms of, an omnipresent underlying malignancy that I call 'sociocultural psychopathology'.[18] In many respects it is like the phenomenon that Freud identified long ago and called 'the pathology of civilized communities', and that the therapist Steven Bartlett recently called 'the pathology of normality'.[19] It has been the principal subject of a number of my previous works, as well as the subject of investigation by others.[20] It is one of the principal topics that will be addressed here.

Most critiques of this complex phenomenon have been rather conventional in that they have relied on familiar psychiatric, psychoanalytical or cognitive-behavioral models. That is, they conceptualized undesirable phenomena as symptoms of one or another kind of pathology that has been categorized in the mainstream mental-health disciplines. For example, the symptoms can be understood as stemming from conflicts between individuals and society at large. (In an old psychoanalytic model, this was the oedipal struggle between the father and his rebellious, ambitious sons.) Or, the culture can be characterized as 'narcissistic' – another traditional (although problematic) type of 'mental disorder'.[21] Just where this pathology of normality or of civilized communities belongs in this scheme of things is a complex matter that will be addressed in due course.

Trying to understand this strange madness in traditional psychiatric or psychoanalytic ways will not do. It leads to the kind of view that Martin Heidegger called 'correct but not true'. This pathology of civilized communities will be envisioned as a radically different kind of pervasive, almost invisible, very serious and quite possibly fatal malady. I will call it simply 'humanity's madness'. As I said, it is not the kind of pathology that is familiar to psychiatrists and other mental-health professionals, although there are ties to familiar nosological categories. It does not appear in the mental-health disciplines' major nosological manuals.[22] A few preparatory chapters are needed before this conception can start to make sense. To paraphrase Wittgenstein, light will need to dawn gradually over the whole[23] – and that 'whole' is quite sizable, so the dawn will take some time.

Characterizing humankind as mad is not likely to be welcomed, even before the import of the label is understood. As Steven Bartlett put it in his interesting and unconventional critique of the common practice of equating mental health with psychological normality,

> Central to human pathology is human resistance to an awareness of it. 'Denial' would be an understatement, for the forces that stand in the way of humankind's reflective consciousness of the psychological and ecological malignancy of the species are incredibly strong, tenacious, and self-preserving.

> As a result of human recalcitrance to acknowledge our own pathology, in the history of behavioral science, and in particular in the history of psychology and psychiatry, almost no effort has been made to gain an understanding of human pathology that has its roots in *normal* – as opposed to abnormal – *psychology*.[24]

An unrecognized, or at best misunderstood, ubiquitous pathology of normality will have developed complex, ubiquitous defensive strategies, and its recognition is almost certain to be ferociously and ubiquitously defended against.

Choosing a starting point

If we want to recast our understanding of the world's dangers as symptoms of a generalized madness, where and how might we begin? Numerous thinkers have told us that the choice of the start is crucial in any exploration. The philosopher Lawrence Cahoone says that

> the question that is most fundamental [is] ... 'What needs to be understood? What requires, calls for, inquiry?' ... the choice of topic, of subject matter, of the issue to be addressed is at least as important as the choice of the basic premises ... The answer to the question 'What calls for my inquiry?' is not imposed on a thinker ... it is grasped in a combination of choice and intellectual vision ... no algorithm, no logic can determine the starting point. It is incorrigibly the product of human intuition, desire, and decision, operating within a historical-cultural context.[25]

The philosopher Frederick Olafson agrees: 'the importance of the decision one makes about where an inquiry is to begin can hardly be overestimated'.[26] Similarly, John Ellis, a professor of German literature, tells us that

> the most important steps in any theoretical inquiry are the initial ones... Whenever a theoretical inquiry fails to begin by looking hard at the position inherited from common thought and practice, the most likely outcome will be a passive acceptance of that position followed by a desperate struggle to deal with its inconsistencies, which, however, never go away.[27]

over kill

Many thinkers also agree that if one expects to make any headway against a problem, one needs to start by taking a close look at the presuppositions that structure the ways in which the problem is usually conceptualized. Thinkers know that many of these presuppositions – usually the ones that are most important – tend to be tacit or latent, making this initial examination extremely difficult. They are instances of what Martin Heidegger called the law of proximity, or, more poetically, referred to as 'the distance of the near': 'the closer we are to something, the harder it is to bring it clearly into view (the lenses on our glasses, for example, or Poe's purloined letter), and thus that the more decisively a matter shapes us, the more difficult it is for us to understand it explicitly'.[28] We can't see the important presuppositions because they are right under our noses.

Wittgenstein expresses a similar view:

> The aspect of things //of language// which are philosophically most important are hidden because of their simplicity and familiarity. One is unable to notice something because it is always (openly) before one's eyes. The real foundation of his inquiry do not strike a man at all. Unless that fact has at some time struck him. And this means he fails to be struck by what is most striking.[29]

Another, related, caveat to keep in mind right from the start, at least according to Heidegger, is that if we want to understand a phenomenon more deeply, we need to be leery of relying on common-sense explanations and understanding. Heidegger

regards the common-sense description of our lives as a distorting lens that warps our deepest understanding of ourselves and our world. The 'self-evidence' and 'obviousness' of common sense is, in his view, the product of a historical shift that culminated in the Enlightenment. 'Common sense,' Heidegger says, is 'the shallow product of that manner of forming ideas which is the final fruit of the eighteenth-century Enlightenment'.[30]

The most recent explorations that have led me to the present perspective suggest that a promising place to start this project is the prevailing view of language, of our normal ideas about what language is and does.[31] That may not be an obvious choice, but nevertheless from my perspective I see it as optimal. I hope to show that when language is considered from certain complex, unfamiliar, unorthodox developmental perspectives, then its exploration will quickly draw most if not all of the issues and concerns relevant to our task into our orbit.

Unavoidable paradoxes

I want to at least mention one other significant and unavoidable difficulty: all explorations and studies of language necessarily rely on language itself. Whether or not it is acknowledged, that self-reference haunts and unsettles any and all explorations of linguistic matters.[32] Thus a vertiginous reflexivity is automatically built into language studies from the start. Language turns back on itself, and/or escapes via an infinite regress. We cannot pin it down; it is a most elusive, strange creature. At times, that innate paradox has been recognized in linguistic inquiries, but in my opinion neither often enough nor deeply enough. Here it will be kept firmly in view. As we will eventually see, the problems raised by language are even worse than that: if by 'studies' we mean what we usually mean, then the study of anything else, too, and not just of language, will necessarily harbor paradoxical self-reference. In other words, the paradoxes of language hemorrhage into the study of anything and everything.

Paradoxical ever-present reflexivity cannot be evaded. It is built into our experiences. In the opening chapter of his work about this phenomenon's ubiquitous, inescapable presence and consequences, Hilary Lawson says:

> Reflexivity, as a turning back on oneself, a form of self-awareness, has been part of philosophy from its inception, but reflexive questions have been given their special force in consequence of the recognition of the central role played by language, theory, sign, and text. Our

concepts are no longer regarded as transparent – either in reflecting the world or conveying ideal. As a result all our claims about language and the world – and implicitly all our claims in general – are reflexive in a manner which cannot be avoided. For to recognize the importance of language is to do so within Language. To argue that the character of the world is in part due to the concepts employed, is to employ those concepts. To insist that we are confined by the limitations of our own problematic, is to be confined within those very limits…such claims as 'there are no facts', there are no lessons of history', 'there are no definitive answers or solutions', are all reflexively paradoxical. For, is it not a fact that 'there are no facts', and a lesson of history that 'there are no lessons of history', and a definitive answer that 'there are no definitive answers'?[33]

Lawson goes on to show how, starting with Nietzsche, the work of radical continental philosophers can be seen as various attempts to get around, deal with or even productively take advantage of this fundamental impediment to secure philosophizing.

The recognition of the inevitable presence and impact of reflexivity has notable precedents. For example, the acknowledgment of reflexivity is implicit in Wittgenstein's famous Tractarian warnings about the ultimate meaninglessness of his propositions, about the need to discard the conceptual ladder that he offers once we have climbed it. He deals with this strange kind of meaninglessness idiosyncratically, whimsically – and paradoxically: 'Don't for heaven's sake, be afraid of talking nonsense! But you must pay attention to your nonsense.'[34] There is some precedent, then, for acknowledging reflexivity in our inquiry, for not covering it up, perhaps even for putting it to work. We will see that such an involvement with reflexivity arises automatically if and when one attends adequately (unconventionally) to certain key ontogenetic and phylogenetic steps. Let us keep that in mind, and begin.

2
What Is Language and Why Does It Matter?

An odd question

What is language? Let us begin by looking at that question itself. Here is what Roy Harris, an Oxford linguist, has to say about it:

> The concept of language is one we take so much for granted that 'What is language?' sounds a very odd question. It is certainly a question which is enough to put any right-minded person on his guard. It is too easily recognized as belonging to that class of bogus inquiries which are justified neither by a genuine desire for information or by social obligation. Leaving aside children, mental defectives and linguistic theorists [I would also include in these exemptions any and all scholars involved in any way in linguistic matters], what a language is is perfectly well understood by anyone who can ask what it is. Accordingly, one who does ask 'What is a language?' must expect to be treated with the same suspicion as the traveller who inquires of the other passengers waiting on Platform I whether any of them can tell him the way to the station.[1]

Not all who think about language have this reaction. Philosophers, linguists, most psychologists and writers are likely to react altogether differently. Ludwig Wittgenstein remarked on this kind of split view, although as usual he did not offer any explanation. His comments were made in the course of discussing the meaning of propositions. He pointed out that raising a question about their nature is likely to seem uninteresting, trivial and tedious to many people; it probably would not even occur to them to ask it. Furthermore, most of us already know what a proposition is – or think we do; just as most of us already know what language is – or think we do. Wittgenstein pointed out the contradiction: 'One person might say: "A proposition is the most ordinary thing in the world" and another: "A proposition – that's something very queer!".'[2] For him, this question which most people regard as ordinary is not only complex but central to philosophy: when one has 'an unassailably true and definitive answer to the question 'what is a proposition?'…one has…solved *all* the problems of philosophy';[3] 'My whole task consists in explaining the nature of the proposition'.[4] At times, Wittgenstein identifies this kind of bifurcation also in other contexts. On one occasion he comments on the differences between the way in which some questions are likely to strike philosophers and non-philosophers. As he does so often in his later work, he draws a picture. He imagines that he is

> sitting with a philosopher in the garden; he says again and again 'I know that that's a tree', pointing to a tree that is near us. Someone else arrives and hears this, and I tell him: 'This fellow isn't insane. We are only doing philosophy.'[5]

One lesson is that, in some contexts at least, we need to be very careful before we dismiss a question as trivial, otiose, even insane, unworthy of consideration. But Wittgenstein also tells us often enough that we need to be careful before we take an issue or question seriously, as meaningful, and begin to pursue it. Examples of this latter case are questions about what he calls 'private language',[6] or conjectures about so-called internal states, such as pains (of which more later).

A similar distinction between commonsense and specialist views is described by the philosopher Charles Guignon in his discussions of Heidegger's philosophical program, and of the Cartesian model of knowledge. He differentiates between situations in which we are trying to gain knowledge of something in the context of 'our actual, everyday predicament' and the more esoteric cases where one is trying to attain some 'highly refined and specialized way of operating in the world'. We need to be aware of whether we are in

> the 'philosophical epistemic situations' characterized in the philosopher's 'common-sense' description of our lives…[or in] the 'plain epistemic situations' of our actual ordinary involvements in the world prior to philosophical reflection.[7]

This is hardly news. We do know, for example, that the ways in which mathematicians see addition is completely different from the way most of us treat arithmetic when we are buying something in a store.

Some situations are much less cut and dried, though. Sometimes assumptions that both experts and non-experts have taken as incontro-vertible, perhaps for a very long time, turn out to be flawed. For instance, one of Einstein's points of departure for the explorations that ulti-mately led him to his revolutionary relativity theory was an apparently frivolous, inconsequential question he asked, one that didn't interest anyone else, that no one before had thought worth asking. In this case, asking it paid huge dividends, of course. It occurred to Einstein to question the apparently quite unproblematic, ordinary, well-understood notion of simultaneity. Everyone knows what 'simultaneous' means – how ridiculous to question it! The rest is history. Simultaneity turned out to be a subtle, surprising, generative notion. Asking what language is is not quite in that lofty league, but I believe that it, too, can lead into productive realms.

The received view of language

How, then, should we approach our odd question about language? To begin with, even if we were to take it seriously, where should we look? To the applicable academic literature? Even a cursory glance at the enormous corpus of relevant explorations in linguistics and philosophy seems to show that at present there are numerous com-peting and hotly debated expert views representing a broad spectrum of sophisticated approaches. There does not seem to be a consensual answer among academicians and professionals. For example, there are major differences between the conceptions of language held by ana-lytic and continental philosophers – say, between Russell's and Frege's views on the one hand, and Heidegger's and Derrida's on the other. However, if we do not intend to be that sophisticated, if all we wish to know (at least for now) is what the chief consensual mainstream beliefs about language are, then the task becomes a good deal more tractable. The differences in the views among philosophers, among *and* casual users dwindle. On the one hand, minor quibbles aside, most scholars hold 'the traditional view of language as a mere instrument for the designation of independently existing entities'.[8] On the other hand, even though most ordinary, non-specialist language users can-not be said to have an explicit theory of language, it is more than likely that even a casual inquiry – say, asking someone to define lan-guage, or what it is – would elicit some response that could be seen as a manifestation of an informal sprawling constellation of latent, implicit beliefs about words, grammar, reference, meaning, definitions and the like. So, although there are apparently great differences between and among the two classes of users (expert and ordinary), there is an underlying broad, mostly unspoken and unrecognized consensus about the nature of language.

John Ellis calls this commonality the 'received view' or 'default condition' of language.[9] He describes it as

the theory with which we all start, the one that is virtually there in the language we speak... the default condition of linguistic theory to which everything reverts when all else fails, as it has seemed to do most of the time: we have a word for cats because cats exist and we need to talk about them and communicate information about them. We have words for the things we want to communicate about cats because the facts we are talking about exist too. Semantics is about matching words to what exists, and syntax and grammar is about a particular language's ordering and structuring the process of communicating these facts. The relation between the world and language is then simply stated. The world has a structure, and language adjusts itself to that structure. It does so imperfectly and untidily, largely because we are an imperfect and untidy species... Theory of language is a field that seems to tempt everyone to begin again conceptually at the beginning... [there is] a widespread sense that no known theory of language works very well... [the received view] is the commonsense point to which we return, over and over again, whenever any attempt to depart from it finally fails.[10]

(But he adds, forebodingly: 'And yet it never works very well either.')

Charles Guignon, writing from a Heideggerian perspective, calls this standard conception the

'name-and-object' model of the workings of language. According to this name-and-object view, language consists of a set of lexical items that are on hand for our use in making assertion or statements about the world. The paradigmatic unit of meaning is the simple predication in which the subject term refers to or picks out some object in the world and the predicate term ascribes some property to it. This picture of language leads us to see the world as made up of so many self-identical things with attributes – the 'substance/accident' ontology.[11]

As I have suggested in an earlier publication,[12] these statements and similar others suggest that the received view of language has the following dominant features:

- it is composed of words (which, in turn, can be broken down into phonemes and graphemes) – one aspect of an atomic view;
- these are building blocks that can be assembled into larger strings, variously called sentences, statements or propositions – another aspect of the atomic view;
- these assemblages follow rules, exhibiting a logical structure that we call grammar, syntax;
- usually, individual words (or longer strings) refer either to non-linguistic entities (things, or thing-like 'somethings') and their properties or attributes, the most common case, or else they can refer to other words or linguistic units, and even (reflexively, self-referentially) to themselves;[13]
- linguistic segments – words, phrases, sentences, paragraphs – 'mean' something (although just what 'meaning' is remains controversial, paradoxical), and such meanings are preserved in correct translations or in synonyms;
- the basic grammatical structure of language strings is the subject/copula/predicate, isomorphic to the item/copula/attribute structure of reality;
- certain kinds of sentence, statement, proposition are either true or false – some tautologically so, others because of one or another real-world fact;
- language is language, regardless of whether it is spoken, written, encoded in abstract symbolic-logical systems, or stored in media such as magnetic tape; its encoded forms are reversible (writing can be read) with only minimal loss, if any;
- language is tool-like, an autonomous object-like entity that can and does perform innumerable varied public tasks and functions such as communicating, informing, describing, referring, arguing, promising, naming, complaining and so on.[14]

The separability assumption

In sum, whether we ask the academician and get a formalized, educated answer, or by skillful, even devious exploratory questioning cull unwittingly held views from naive users, I believe that these properties capture the essentials of the view of language that is embedded in our culture: Ellis's 'received view'.

Language is a self-contained, autonomous atomic semiotic system. Its branches are semantics, having to do with meanings; syntactics, having to do with rules that govern its structure; and pragmatics, having to do with its utility to user or agents. It is made up of identifiable 'elementary particles' (its 'atomic' aspect) that link up according to the rules of grammar and the demands of reality to form larger elements (nouns, verbs, phonemes – 'strings'). The atoms are classifiable according to some logical scheme (nouns, verbs, adjectives) and capable of being assembled into ever larger, more complex meaningful strings (clauses, sentences, paragraphs, books) as dictated by various kinds of syntactic rule. This system is an independent tool that has floated free from its users. It can be used to describe, name, refer, define, promise, swear and so on.

As has been adumbrated, even from this ordinary, cursory look one can see that there is something a bit odd about language: although it can become an excisable, isolated, decontextualized object of study in disciplines such as logic, linguistics, paradoxically, in such situations it serves both as that autonomous object of a discipline's study and simultaneously also as the tool used by that discipline to study that very entity. In part because of this paradoxical, self-reflexive dualism, some critics have challenged the claim that linguistics is, or can be, a science.[15] The argument is that the reflexive paradox that such a discipline would necessarily entail makes the notion of an 'objective' scientific study of language incoherent. (I believe that the paradox necessarily underlies all enterprises, although it may be more difficult to spot in some than in others. The argument against linguistics could be applied to any other apparently objective field – logic, for example).[16] In countless instances, though, it nevertheless has been the object of scientific inquiry, logical analysis and formal theorizing. Thus in spite of the mind-boggling lurking reflexivity, in all important respects it is treated much like any other object that is deemed to be a legitimate target of scientific investigation.

For instance, the linguist Daniel Everett's study of the Pirahã Amazon tribe (of which much more later) gives many examples of such a typical objectified, scientific treatment of language.[17] Everett says that, as a scientist, objectivity is one of his most deeply held values. Almost every page of his report about his life with the Pirahã demonstrates that, and how, mainstream linguistics turns language-in-use-by-persons-in-a-world into an object suitable for normal science's (Kuhn's term) exploration.[18] The basic tasks of scientists' field studies are data collection, storage and analysis. Meaning becomes objectified, depersonalized: 'in an nutshell: the way a word or a sentence is used, the way it relates to other words and sentences, and what speakers agree that a word or a sentence points to in the world'.[19] So, as the philosopher Frederick Olafson puts it, in general the world's received view of language

> takes for granted that language use is an overt and observable function of the human organism and thus takes its place unproblematically within the same natural milieu as all the other processes with which the sciences are concerned…It tends to be simply assumed that language, particularly its distinctive semantic and referential functions, presents no special problem for a naturalistic account of human nature.

Olafson adds that 'Through an effective separation of language from its users and their distinctive mode of being in the world, all questions about the ontological status of language itself may be elided and even never raised at all.'[20] This separation quickly and easily leads to the illusion that language is a potent entity that all by itself can accomplish certain aims on its own, just as pure mathematics and logic tends to make it seem that proofs somehow evolve from axiomatic grounds that somehow have materialized out of thin air. Attempts to bring the person, the mathematician, into the picture are rejected, disdained as unacceptable 'psychologizing'.[21] Mathematics is 'out there', Platonic, waiting to be discovered, not made. In reality, numbers, language and subjectivity are tightly interwoven, inseparable.[22] Once again, the received view, in this case of mathematics, is distorted enormously by conveniently forgetting the considerable, century- if not millennia-long amount of prior stage-setting that has gone into this apparently depersonalized atemporal activity. Even the more current aspects of this preparatory stage-setting, such as the years of study and training of the mathematicians themselves, remain out of sight.

I have called the belief that language is an autonomous object-like entity the 'separability assumption'.[23] We will see that it has a range of applications. It is not confined to the study of language; its noxious effects are widespread. In the context of language, the result is that language 'may be said to have floated free of any ground it may have been supposed to have in the world',[24] the stage-setting forgotten. Detaching and isolating an entity in this fashion, divorcing it from its history, grossly distorts it, leads to fallacious thinking and all too often to the pursuit of meaningless questions. (This is how the sciences' 'view from nowhere' arises.)[25] In Wittgenstein's calling attention to prior stage-setting we have a rare example of a philosopher who is raising what is essentially a developmental issue, pointing out that a situation has a history, and that that history is relevant (but for Wittgenstein, only up to a point, as we will see). The evacuation of the person from the scene is a feature not only of the default view of language but also of its associated received view of world. It is the classically scientific stance: 'the first prerequisite Descartes lays out for his method of inquiry...is that we disengage ourselves from our active involvement in the world in order to achieve the vantage point of an unprejudiced spectator'[26] – not only unprejudiced but absent. The absent spectator who nevertheless is able to observe, use language, report, injects yet another paradox into the usual, unexamined view of self, world and language.

For more than a century this disregard of context, the splitting of persons and their world, especially this kind of severing and excision that is an essential feature of science (think of all the commotion about brain studies),[27] has been the target of radical philosophical reformers with holistic ambitions, even though the received view and its separability assumption continue to reign. For example, 'One of Heidegger's goals in *Being and Time* is to diagnose and deflate the picture of the self as a substantial subject distinct from an external world of things.'[28] The linguist Roy Harris has roundly criticized this separatist, objectifying conception of language that is so prevalent in his field. He calls it the 'segregationist view', and wants to replace it with the view he calls 'integrationist', a term that he chose

> to reflect the notion that communication systems, including languages like English, exist independently not only of one another but of how they may – or may not – be used by those who use them...[Segregationism adopts] a perspective in which a language becomes detached, as it were, from its speakers...The notion that the product has an internal structure *of its own* which in the end depends neither on the producer nor on the production process is the segregational assumption that became the key to analyzing all verbal manifestations of *logos*. Once this happens, speech is no longer the whole it once was.[29]

The received view of the world

We can glimpse that although it is far from obvious, one's views of what language is and does are closely tied to a set of corresponding views about one's self and one's world, a world that paradoxically and vertiginously includes that self: the constellation of beliefs that from now on I will call simply 'worldview'. What worldview, then, corresponds to, is linked to, the received view of language? A typical version is the one that the philosopher Charles Taylor calls the Hobbes–Locke–Condillac theory – the set of ideas developed from Locke through Hobbes to Condillac. The received view of language harbors a theory that

> seeks to understand language within the confines of the modern representational epistemology made dominant by Descartes. In the mind there are 'ideas.' These are bits of putative representation of reality, much of it 'external.' Knowledge consists in having representation actually square with the reality. But we can only hope to achieve this if we assemble our ideas according to a responsible procedure. Our beliefs about things are constructed; they result from a synthesis. The issue is whether the construction will be reliable and responsible, or indulgent, slapdash, and delusory. Language plays an important role in this construction.[30]

This epistemological/ontological picture implicit in the received view of language is compatible with Roy Harris's description of the analogous mainstream worldview that results from what he calls 'the language myth', the dogma that

> Words are items belonging to a conventionally agreed linguistic code, shared by all members of a linguistic community. This code allegedly functions as a system enabling one member of the community to exchange thoughts with any other member who understands the code. Thanks to this, *A* can know what *B* thinks (provided *B* has used the code correctly to express these thoughts). The alleged process of codified thought-transference I call 'telementation'...These linguistic assumptions...underlie the whole enterprise of Western science and scientific education, including mathematics...I shall distinguish between two views of meaning associated with the language myth. On one view, words get their meanings by 'standing for' ideas in the mind: I call this the *psychocentric* version of the myth. On the other view, words get their meanings by 'standing for' things in the 'real world' outside the mind. I call this the *reocentric* version of the myth.[31]

Just what it is that brings about the close coupling between the two received views (language and world) is difficult to say. (We will find out more in Chapter 3 when we consider the phenomenon of first language acquisition.) That may be so, but the tie exists nevertheless:

Philosophy has become mired in the question of language because although the importance of the relationship between language and the world cannot be evaded, no credible account of that relationship has been forthcoming. Realists have been unable to give an explanation as to how language refers to the world; while non-realists have found themselves trapped in language unable to account for how it has content, or how it is possible to say anything at all.[32]

In spite of these difficulties it seems to be widely accepted in philosophy that our received view of language leads quite naturally to a dualistic view of the world.[33] Heidegger has written extensively about the connections between our usual conception of language as thing-like and our essentially Cartesian conception of world. It is science's picture. Heidegger calls it by different names such as 'technological' or 'rational-calculative thinking', 'enframing'.[34] He makes a complex move: he takes this relatively recent worldview, the view that has dominated Western thought since the emergence of modern science, and sets it within a much larger historical conceptual framework that he calls 'ontotheology' – an offputting term: 'On hearing the expression "ontotheology," many philosophers [and just about all others too] start looking for the door.'[35] This problematic term and position which Heidegger sometimes also called 'metaphysics', 'subjectivism', 'humanism' has been extensively discussed and debated in the secondary Heideggerian literature. The sketch that follows is bound to seem like a travesty or sacrilege to scholars but it will have to do for our limited purposes.

As I see it, then, the term 'ontotheology' reflects a way of understanding, systematizing and finally unifying the 2000-plus-year history of the apparently changing constellations of beliefs about world and self that have characterized Western philosophical thought since ancient Greece. Heidegger organizes this procession of seemingly disparate beliefs into five 'epochs': 'pre-Socratic, Platonic, medieval, modern, and (our own) late-modern epochs'.[36] Each lasted some centuries, each exhibited its own interlocking idiosyncratic set of beliefs and assumptions, yet in spite of their apparent differences and idiosyncrasies, according to Heidegger there is an underlying commonality, a two-element structure. Each epoch's system of beliefs has the same two kinds of basic conceptual ingredients – the same underlying metaphysics. One of these belief clusters, the 'ontological' aspect (the 'onto' in ontotheology), comprises beliefs about what there is, what the world's ingredients are. For us, in our epoch, that essentially is what the natural sciences provide. They tell us what the world's furniture is – and a baffling story it is. The second class of ingredients are the 'theological' – roughly, beliefs about the kinds of transcendental questions, realities and issues that concern theology, some philosophy, mysticism, new-age thinking, even non-traditional psychiatry.[37] The first kind of entities explain the world from the inside as it were, how we see the world when we, from inside it, look out at it. The second kind of ingredients explain the world as seen from the outside, from a God's-eye view or similar other-worldly, transcendent perspective.

According to Heidegger, then, our technological thinking is just the latest, current version of the five ontological epochs. Heidegger identifies and discusses it at great length, and his views about it have generated a substantial secondary literature.[38] I want to point to the connections that Heidegger makes between our current view of language and our approach to our world:

> In the technological mode of cultural attunement, 'framing,' [another term for rational-calculative thinking] according to Heidegger, man's attempt to gain domination over the world by grounding it in a self-grounding ground takes the shape of formalizing language in 'information theory.' The quest for formalized language, says Heidegger, 'is the metaphysics of the thorough-going technicalization of all languages to the sole functioning instrument of interplanetary information.' When language has been formalized, it may then be regarded as a posit of man, on hand for his use in achieving mastery over the world.[39]

In this context, Heidegger offers a great deal of complex, often obscure and ambiguous thought about this current worldview that he characterizes as technological thinking. We must remember that he does not use this term in its usual sense. For him, as he repeats so insistently, the essence of technological thinking is not technology per se – not science and the various technological advances and physical products and gadgets that it makes possible. I want to point out, though, that what Heidegger sees as the most undesirable consequences of framing (or 'enframing') or technological thinking differs greatly in at least one important respect from my view. The drastic costs he saw incurred by this position were

> the human distress caused by the *technological understanding of being*, rather than the destruction caused by technology – ecological

Grof

destruction, nuclear danger, consumerism, etc. – from the devastation that would result if technology solved all our problems... The
'greatest danger' is that 'the approaching tide of technological revolution in the atomic age could so captivate, bewitch, dazzle, and beguile
man that calculative thinking may someday come to be accepted and
practiced *as the only way* of thinking.'[40]

This is not at all what I see as enframing's most nefarious, dangerous
aspect. It amounts to a difference in values. Heidegger's concerns were a
philosopher's, and I suppose that makes his priorities if not acceptable
then at least understandable. I believe that my concerns and priorities
are those that are held by most non-philosophers: from the perspective
of a human being, matters pertaining to the world's devastation have an
obvious, unquestionable priority. Global survival seems immeasurably
more significant and imperative than any specialist priority advocated
within an academic field such as philosophy. That seems beyond dispute. I find Heidegger's priorities appalling and difficult to understand,
even though he is a philosopher. But then, as I have said several times by
now, I am not. I do believe, though, that his challenging the assumption
that technology (in his wide sense) can solve our problems is a valuable one, though counterintuitive and liable to raise opposition. The
assumption is profoundly dangerous. More of that later.

His critique of technological thinking contains much that is valuable. Briefly, in Heidegger's views, 'technology' has two facets, as any
era's metaphysics is postulated to have in his ontotheological schema.
According to him, then, the first aspect, the 'onto' pole, is our view of
ourselves as centers of the universe, the position Heidegger labels and
condemns as 'humanism', 'individualism' or 'subjectivism'. Its second
feature is our 'technological' orientation, a complex aspect of technological thinking that according to Heidegger takes everything, ourselves
included, as something potentially transformable into useful energy, in
Heidegger's terminology into 'standing-reserve'. Everything, ourselves
included, is transformed into, and becomes treated as, lifeless glorified
fuel in a supply depot. We must remember what he so strongly and
almost constantly emphasizes: the 'essence' of technological thinking is
not technology – at least not technology as we think of it. In Heidegger's
usage, technology does not refer to the gadgets, weapons, practices and
methodologies that seem to pose the immediate dangers, but rather
to their tacitly underlying dehumanizing, rapacious, alienating toxic
framework with its values and assumptions. Enframing entails a position of dominance and full mastery over everything – amoral, brutal,

exploitive, destructive, callous – leading to our becoming what the psychoanalyst Joel Kovel calls the enemy of nature.[41] I consider the other, '-theological', pole below.

State process formalisms

I arrived at a broadly consonant but much simpler alternative to enframing from an engineer-psychologist's orientation. I came to see the core of our technological thinking as a grounding in a ubiquitous implicit and explicit, depersonalizing and depersonalized, logical-mathematical formalism – namely, the framework into which we formally or informally, deliberately or unawares, cast just about any and all phenomena and experiences.[42] In terms of that alternative to Heidegger's model, we do not put everything in a gas tank. Instead, we conceptualize all in terms of a class of mathematical structures, and treat it accordingly. Under that view, the essence of 'technologizing', of rational-technological thinking, is the particular perspective that is imposed on our conceptions of self and world when we have structured them in terms of the properties of the mathematical model or constellation that decades ago I called 'state process formalisms' – roughly, the scientific reductionistic, determinist, depersonalized arid model already conceptualized by the late eighteenth-century mathematician the Marquis de Laplace:

> We may regard the present state of the universe as the effect of its past and the cause of its future. An intellect which at a certain moment would know all forces that set nature in motion, and all positions of all items of which nature is composed, if this intellect were also vast enough to submit these data to analysis, it would embrace in a single formula the movements of the greatest bodies of the universe and those of the tiniest atom; for such an intellect nothing would be uncertain and the future just like the past would be present before its eyes.[43]

In a more contemporary version, this formal structure provides the armature for conceptualizing any and all situations. (Typically, that imposition of structure passes unnoticed.) State process formalisms conceptualize 'situations' as states of systems, and their 'changes' as changes of state that occur in response to and in accordance with specified forces and rules. Then, systems and their states can be geometrically modeled. The system (the scientific representation of something in the world – perhaps something that is outside us, perhaps something in our 'inner world') becomes a point located in a multidimensional (n-dimensional) space whose coordinates represent the system's properties (location, velocity, temperature, anxiety, degree of arousal and so on). Then the system's changing states are represented by the path that the point takes through the coordinate space. Its changing locations mean that its coordinate values are changing, and these represents the system's changing states, properties, attributes.[44] Usually, but not always, not necessarily, the movement of the point/system is a movement that is occurring over time. The path that the system takes is governed by rules and laws that some theory has postulated. This model is the formalism that is invariably used in the natural sciences. It underlies thought in physics from Newton to Bohr and Einstein. Although sometimes it may be difficult to discern its underlying presence, as far as I know it is used in formal scientific work to represent every phenomenon. It has become so familiar to natural scientists and technologists that it is scarcely noticed, yet, strangely enough, it is almost an anomaly in psychology, as I discovered to my surprise.[45] For me, this formalism is the 'onto-' part of our present version of metaphysics: ontotheology.

I am less certain about what currently constitutes its '-theology' part. My best guess is that it is the 'scientific spirit' – that is, the constellation comprising science's beliefs and dogmas – its realism assumptions,[46] its rationalism, values and ethics, methodologies, sanctioned practices, its scientism. This spirit dictates that all can and needs to be quantified, formalized, mathematized, validated, observed impersonally and objectively; that one must militantly guard against psychologism or the injection of any other non-material, non-physicalistic perspective; and paradoxically, while denying that it is dualistic, this scientific spirit nevertheless covertly clings to Cartesian dualism. That seems to me to be the current form of the external-deity pole of our logocentrism.

The spirit of state formalisms dominates our culture in general. It is the mostly tacit, covert, unrecognized armature that structures our articulated conception of self and world. Wittgenstein seems to be one of the very few thinkers who recognized its presence. He not only recognized it but also had an acute sense of the importance that this formal model assumed in our thinking. Most especially, he recognized the undesirable consequences that follow its use in certain contexts, ones in which this formalization that occurs so automatically is not only inappropriate but also pernicious. He made the following general remarks in the course of a critique of taking language about 'inner mental events' as referential (we refer to pains, rules and so on):

> How does the philosophical problem about mental processes and states and about behaviorism arise? – The first step is the one that altogether escapes notice. We talk of processes and states, and we leave their nature undecided. Sometime perhaps we shall know more about them – we think. But that is just what commits us to a particular way of looking at this matter. For we have a definite concept of what it means to know a process better. (The decisive movement in the conjuring trick has been made, and it is the very one that we thought was quite innocent.)[47]

Wittgenstein implies that we don't know what mental processes and states are, and that therefore when we think or say that we are explaining these via the notion of a state, we are what he often calls 'gassing'. We are raising Berkeleyan dust and then complaining that we cannot see. To my knowledge, this highly insightful, important critique of the notion of state has fallen between the cracks. I have never seen it discussed, appreciated or even mentioned, certainly not in psychology and related disciplines. The use of state notions when talking about inner events remains as ubiquitous as ever (and still mostly unexamined, overlooked). I believe it can even be shown to undergird formal theories in linguistics, such as Noam Chomsky's transformational grammar.

This chapter has sketched the received view of 'language' and argued that it is tightly coupled to a corresponding received view of 'world' – indeed, that the two are barely, if at all, distinguishable. Let us next begin to consider developmental issues. Chapter 3 sketches a model of individual human development (ontogenesis), with an emphasis on the mind-boggling, yet paradoxically taken-for-granted phenomenon, of first language acquisition – an ontogenetic phenomenon. It, like language itself, is ubiquitous, an everyday occurrence, mistakenly considered to be routine and unremarkable – a considerable underestimation. Chapter 4 will do much the same for another kind of linguistic developmental acquisition, a cultural one (phylogenetic) – namely, humanity's acquisition of literacy.

3
Infancy and First Language Acquisition

We have examined one class of views about language, what it is and does, a family of beliefs we called the received or default view. I mentioned that it has long been criticized for its severe internal difficulties. The view raises baffling questions and paradoxes, is tied to a basically incoherent worldview, and so on. Nevertheless, it has maintained dominance, mostly because no viable alternative has emerged, at least not so far. I see this failure to offer a viable alternative as closely tied to the near-total absence of any serious interest in the first steps of the infant's acquisition of their language in those disciplines that concern themselves with language in general (linguistics, philosophy, psychology, psychiatry). This chapter will explain the nature of this surprising link between world view and first language acquisition.

The paradox

How do infants acquire their first language? Although the literature is large, 'the topic is one without a discipline. There are virtually no university departments of language acquisition...and only one major journal is devoted to it.'[1] There is no shortage of theories, but, as far as I can see, all are based on one or another kind of cognitive behavioral model. Vygotsky and Piaget set the standard.[2] In psychology, linguistics, philosophy, pedagogy, the mental health fields, education, the prevalent belief is that each infant's acquisition of their mother tongue (the logician W. V. O. Quine calls it the 'home language') is a relatively unremarkable, everyday phenomenon that can be scientifically or logically investigated and understood. Unless there is something wrong with the infant, of course each child learns the language of their culture. It happens, we can explain it scientifically, and that's all there's to it. Children learn language in much the same way as they learn to walk, to read and write, to do arithmetic. Occasionally one may find a dissenting view, but it fails to gain traction. The literature is sizable so I cannot be sure that I haven't missed some relevant work, but the only philosophers I know who have gone beyond a superficial, inadequate view are Charles Taylor and, to a minor degree, Wittgenstein. (I am not aware of any comparable work by psychologists, psychiatrists, or linguists.) I draw heavily on Taylor's analyses, especially in the earlier parts of this chapter.

I suppose one reason why this blasé perception has become the received view of language acquisition is that it fits our reductive, over-simplifying, mechanizing general attitudes and practices so well. It also may be, though, because to confront this phenomenon seriously is to run headlong into paradox, as Wittgenstein and a few others (for example, the philosopher Johann Gottfried von Herder) have found.[3] I strongly disagree with the received opinion, often masquerading as fact, that language acquisition is understandable, a suitable phenomenon for scientific study or else of relatively little significance. I see the process as important and utterly baffling. I'm not alone. I have already mentioned Wittgenstein; the English professor and literary critic Ian Robinson is another. In the course of his extended critical study of Noam Chomsky's language theories, he says that

> The study of language is one mode of contemplating a mystery, and a proper awe is a measure of the sense and depth of what goes on in the study of language. I mean, not that linguists should talk about their wonder and awe or use it to gain recruits to the profession…but that awe at language should be present in linguistics and inform it…Children begin to understand what is said to them and to talk. All children. That is a wonder of the world – of the specifically human world.[4]

The specialness and paradoxical nature of this infant accomplishment can be explained superficially, but not satisfactorily. One way or another, one always bumps up against the problem of origins, against the paradoxes entailed in Leibniz's Principle of Reason – *nihil est sine ratione* ('nothing is without reason').[5] How do we account for the start of the way in which we account for the start of something?[6] Trying to explain first language acquisition deeply raises the specter of infinite regress. The explanation will have to be explained. We can infer that Wittgenstein considered the process important because he opens his *Philosophical Investigations* with St. Augustine's account of how he acquired his mother tongue. Wittgenstein immediately makes this salient comment:

These words, it seems to me, give us a particular picture of the essence of human language. It is this: the individual words in language name objects – sentences are combinations of such names. – In this picture of language we find the roots of the following idea: Every word has a meaning. The meaning is correlated with the word. It is the object for which the word stands.[7]

He is pointing out that our conception of how infant language acquisition occurs is coupled to our conception of (the adult's) language (his description of that conception is essentially an abstract of the received view) – surely a startling and important connection, especially in view of the further connection that I pointed out in Chapter 2 (that our conception of 'adult language' is tightly yoked to our conception of the world as well – that the ties are reciprocal, bilateral). So, the further implication of Wittgenstein's remark is that our conceptualization of first language acquisition has a great deal to do with our conception of 'world' and 'self' – a momentous insight. Yet, although from his remark it seems obvious that Wittgenstein was well aware of the importance of this event – else why open this important work by considering it? – he offers no explanation for it. He has no 'theory of first language acquisition' (just as he has no theory of language). He limits himself to offering a critique of St. Augustine's report of how he learned to speak. Basically, it is the commonsense view of the process as explainable by ostension, essentially that the child learns the meanings and definitions of words and sentences by adults' pointing (in a broad sense), coupling sight (or some surrogate) and sound, joining use and definition – saying: 'we call *this* (pointing) an apple'. That model of first language learning remains our current received wisdom.

Wittgenstein goes on to show that explaining first language learning by ostension is untenable:

Thus, we can see Augustine's tendency to think of the human subject in terms of a private essence or mind – in which there are determinate wishes, thoughts, desires, and so on – and a physical interface with the outside world... The private essence is conceived as somehow already fully human,[8] but as lacking the capacity to communicate with others. It already possesses its own internal articulations into particular thoughts and wishes, which cannot yet be expressed... Within Augustine's account of how we come to acquire language, there is contained the idea of a completed, or structured, human consciousness inside the child, which exists prior to the child's acquisition of language....the child acquires language in order to express the thoughts and wishes that are already there inside him. Augustine describes this process in such a way that the child is credited with an innate insight into the technique of assigning names to things...Wittgenstein suggests that Augustine describes the child's learning his first language as if he were a foreigner coming into a strange country [language acquisition is just like the adult's or older child's *second-language* learning][9] ...Any sense that the account of language acquisition that Augustine presents somehow *explains* how we learn language is thus shown to be an illusion. For the picture actually presupposes that it purports to explain.[10]

The absence of any alternative is telling. Wittgenstein offers none. Instead, he says that the issue should be removed from philosophy, stating unequivocally that 'The *process* of learning does not matter [for philosophy only?]; it is history and history does not matter here...[A] claim as to how we learn language seems curiously out of place in a philosophical discussion'.[11] (Presumably it belongs elsewhere – but where?) He passes the buck. He not only sidesteps explaining first language acquisition, but immediately turns to the use of language by older children and adults, illuminating this much later use of language with his concepts of language games and forms of life. He thus has left behind the first language acquisition issues.

It is important to recognize that what is wrong with the idea that it is ostensive learning that leads an infant to first couple ordinary things and words, is also wrong with the way we believe that the child learns to talk about their events – wishes, thoughts, feelings. The common view is that the child learns to name them, talk about them, refer to them also via varieties of ostensive teaching and learning. In a complex, extended series of remarks (including his vertiginous critique of the idea he calls 'private language'), Wittgenstein shows that this notion, too, is unsustainable. Whatever it is that is going on in what we call our inner world, to talk about it referentially as though we were describing actual objects is untenable, at least in the case of the child who is just beginning to talk.[12] [more in ch. 4]

Wittgenstein's critique of the Augustinian picture has an interesting precursor. In the eighteenth century, the French philosopher and epistemologist Etienne Bonnot de Condillac offered a similarly ostension-based explanation of the origins of language. He imagines the fanciful scene of two isolated children who together learn to speak all by themselves, and uses it to explain first language acquisition. The philosopher Johann Gottfried Herder challenged Condillac's theory, claiming that it was circular, question-begging. Herder argued that explaining the emergence of language in a child by means of an ostensive theory of learning presupposed precisely what it claimed to explain – exactly Wittgenstein's objection to Augustine's explanation. That is, one already has to know that ostension establishes meaning in order to learn that it does so. The theory could work only by assuming what it purported to set out to explain.[13]   *Charles*

At the time, Herder's was a radical critique. Taylor says that for Herder

> to raise this issue is to swing our perspective on language into a new angle. But it's easy to miss. Condillac was unaware that he had left anything out. He wouldn't have known where Herder was 'coming from,' just as his heirs today, the proponents of chimp language, talking computers, and truth-conditional theories of meaning, find the analogous objections to their views gratuitous and puzzling.[14]

Taylor also points out that Herder did not, apparently could not, resolve this chicken-or-egg circularity. He, just like Wittgenstein, offered no alternative and, also like Wittgenstein, just abandoned the subject. It is striking that although both saw the flaws in the ostensive theory of language acquisition, neither one of these unconventional critics could offer a viable alternative. Surely that says something about the elusiveness of the phenomenon.

I am convinced that the inability of either of these thinkers to say more about the process stems from their philosopher's lack of understanding of early child development. Herder had nowhere to turn to learn more about it, but Wittgenstein did have a considerable body of relevant psychoanalytic literature available. Although he read Freud and offered criticisms of psychoanalysis,[15] Wittgenstein gives no indication that he is aware of the complex psychoanalytic conceptualizations of ontogenesis, let alone of their considerable clinical import. His views and critiques of psychoanalysis lack clinical acumen; they address the undisputed weaknesses of its theories from the standpoint of a logician.[16] His capacity to understand what is valuable in psychoanalysis apparently was limited by his philosopher's perspective, a myopia that remains ubiquitous among academic critics of psychoanalysis to this day.[17]

Quine, too, points to the far-reaching importance of the phenomenon of first language acquisition. He notes the connection between what he calls 'the classical picture of language acquisition' and 'traditional epistemology', referring to the

> setting up of some kind of cognitive or psychological connection between individual words and corresponding elements of the speaker's physical environment, mental life, or sense experience, which then become recognized as the 'meanings' or 'designata' of the words in question. This is the classical picture of language acquisition as a methodical, deliberate, and linear process, beginning with the direct apprehension of the 'meanings' of a few simple and discrete linguistic elements and rules of combination and proceeding step by step to a full master/of the infinite variety and complexity of all linguistic forms in a language. This picture of language acquisition is also at the root of traditional epistemology.[18]

Thus Quine, like Wittgenstein, explicitly recognizes the intimate ties between the standard picture of first language acquisition and the standard epistemological tradition. It seems reasonable to generalize this link to other pairs of language acquisition theories and associated epistemologies (I would include ontologies). This speculation is supported indirectly by Quine's views about the general indeterminacy of translation and inscrutability of reference, including his radical opinion that 'a certain 'dimness of reference' ... can be found lingering even in our own 'home' language'.[19] He is implying that, paradoxically, one never knows what one is talking about in any context, in any language, no matter how acquired – surely a momentous admission, and very much in line with the views to be developed here.

I plan to demonstrate that leaving behind the received view of language and its entailed ontoepistemology/worldview necessitates having a conception of first language acquisition that differs radically from the traditional explanations and beliefs. Again, I am convinced that this entire subject area, the broad questions about the nature of language and about worldviews (what I call our 'ontoepistemology'), cannot be dealt with adequately without introducing relevant aspects of the ontogenetic and phylogenetic dimensions. One must somehow come to terms with the problem of origins.

Learning theories

Why is there this tight coupling between concepts of language acquisition and epistemology/ontology? The ties may be acknowledged, intuited, but they are rarely explained. One exception is Charles Taylor's instructive hypothesis. He ties a pair of antithetical learning theories to a parallel, corresponding pair of antithetical conceptions of language. That is, each learning theory is tied to a corresponding conception of language. He adds a third pair of antithetical views, different ways of conceptualizing one's being in the world, and again links each view to one of the preceding linked pairs. We thus have three polarized pairs, and one member of each is linked with corresponding members in the other two pairs. This may seem confusing, but it is simple: one learning theory, one corresponding conception of language, and one corresponding worldview are tied together, and we have two such sets of correlated triplets.[20]

Taylor labels the pair of contrastive learning theories 'genetic' and 'incremental', and the corresponding contrasting pair of language conceptions 'expressive/constitutive' and 'designative'. Genetic learning theories are linked to expressive/constitutive theories of language (not invariably, but almost always), while incremental learning theories are linked to designative theories of language. (The pair of contrasting worldviews – the third of these pairs – will be considered later.)

Genetic learning theories belong to 'a certain field within psychology' which Taylor, naturally enough, calls 'genetic' psychology. It is a minority field because it holds

> the view that there is a special complex of problems of ontogenesis. That goes against the [majority] view that sees growth . . . as explicable by very non-specific mechanisms. The major antagonist to a genetic psychology is thus an *incremental* view of learning.[21]

It is this antagonist to genetic theories, the incremental learning model, that has dominated Anglo-Saxon psychology for some time.[22] Of the pair of learning models (genetic and incremental) it is primarily the incremental theories that are compatible with and conform to the standards of normal science (Thomas Kuhn).

In incremental learning models, growth takes place more or less smoothly, continuously. The ontology and epistemology remain Cartesian. Each apparently new stage of development is seen as 'a specific differential concatenation of the same fundamental building blocks',[23] a rearrangement of the ingredients found in the preceding state. This, incidentally, is an excellent illustration of what in general I have called the 'adultocentric position': it assumes that the newborn develops more or less smoothly, continuously, into the adult.[24] The most obvious inference is that, in that sense, although there are readily apparent and undeniable differences, the child is much like an adult.

(Although the implication is rarely considered, this model also implies that the adult is much like an infant.) It is like an adult to begin with, and remains like an adult until it obviously *is* an adult. This is a widely held view of infancy, expressed in mainstream science's conception of the young child as 'the competent infant' (see below). Apparent exceptions, such as Piaget's conception of stages, are just that – in critical aspects, only apparent, as we shall soon see.

That is not the view of development conceptualized under the opposed genetic view. The patterns of intelligence, learning, emotional life and so on are distinctly different for each phase of childhood. Unlike in the incremental learning models, each new phase exhibits changes in kind. Growth is not smooth, but a succession of discontinuous, even disruptive states in which new elements appear and old ones may disappear. (I would add that, in true genetic theories, the underlying ontology changes as well. It is because in supposedly genetic theories, such as Piaget's, the ontology remains essentially the same – the ontology that underlies cognitive behaviorism – that I do not consider them to be true genetic theories, but rather incremental theories in disguise.) These abrupt changes happen, if not instantaneously, at least very quickly. Growth is fundamental transformation. Let us examine each of these two complex pictures more closely and see how they affect our views of language acquisition and maturation in general.

The competent infant and incremental learning

Let us first consider how incremental learning theories conceptualize very young infants – what they can do, how they do it, what they are experiencing – in short, in terms of Thomas Nagel's question about bats, 'what it is like' to be a newborn.[25] There is a broad consensus, supposedly experimentally/empirically supported and thus 'scientifically verified', that in important essentials the newborn, and perhaps to some extent even the fetus, is much like an adult. The young baby may be primitive, primordial, but nevertheless it has some important rudiments of an adult's capacities, albeit in a nascent and/or primal form. Even in the first few post-natal months, it already is 'the little scientist' (Piaget) investigating the world. My point is that holding this belief prejudices observations and makes one's findings a foregone conclusion. If they believe the competent infant model, then all that empirical investigators of infancy would be able to observe is bound to bear out their hypothesis of the competent infant; it is a self-fulfilling prophecy. The observers' interpretations of their so-called data (which already are interpretations of physical movements or sounds – for example, scientists record that the baby 'cries', and not that it emits an acoustic signal of this or that frequency, intensity and duration) will be consonant with our ordinary commonsense views of infancy – that is, with our current commonsense views.[26] The reasoning is simple and compelling: child development and learning is incremental; there are no discontinuities;[27] the child becomes an adult; therefore it must have been adult-like from the very beginning. (Genetics, neurobiology, instinct theory and so on can then explain this innate foundation or constancy.) And, besides, one can *see* that when the child, say, cries, it is in pain, or hungry, or at least uncomfortable. Who would question such observations? Well – I, for one.

Here are some scientific claims that are representative of incremental learning theorizing about infants:

[The neonate's suckling responses] entail perception... [infants can make] perceptual discriminations... Here is a perception that is selective with respect to the stimuli... a response that requires a set of rules in the infant about patterns which are of interest or matter... Here is a process that most would describe as psychological and yet at a relatively low level of sophistication. It undoubtedly involves intentional causality.... Infants show clearly that they enjoy contact with other people... We have seen already that even at a few weeks of age infants are able to participate in joint activities with caregivers in which there are shared rules of engagement... Increasingly non-verbal communication, and communication about communication, is joined... the selection among multiple sets of rules may be linked to consciousness within the agent, and to language... Notwithstanding the evident, great differences between intentionality [roughly, directed consciousness] in the beginnings of life and in the mature human mind, the transitions are seamless;[28] ... One can reasonably claim that pre-linguistic infants can have beliefs and act on the basis of reasons... infants appear to recognize, discriminate, investigate, re-identify and classify, and all this without the aid of language;[29] ... It would be foolish to deny that infants and animals feel fear or anger;[30] ... Even in the cradle, babies as young as 5 months have a rudimentary ability to add and subtract, according to a study being published today;[31] ... [Newborns can] pick out mother's face from a gallery of photos, are mentally curious and eager to learn, recognize the gender of other babies.... [they are] small creatures with unexpectedly large thoughts.[32]

chamberlain 1998
your new born baby

Such beliefs are ubiquitous in the applicable scientific literature. The examples offered in their support here can be multiplied at will.[33]

These views of the neonate are supported by commonsense, everyday experience, and we are told also by evidence gained in formal, scientifically rigorous empirical studies conducted by competent, credible experimental, developmental and clinical psychologists, pedagogues, neurobiologists, psycholinguists and anthropologists. The views are also supported by the rarely questioned principle of Leibniz mentioned earlier, the principle of reason – the adultocentrism-supporting dogma that nothing is without reason: *nihil est sine ratione*.[34] If a young child can do arithmetic, that ability must have been there in some form from the start. That, and a host of other expectations like it, inevitably prejudice the scientific observer.

As I have suggested, perhaps the most powerful support for this conception of infancy comes from the tacitly held dogma that a child's growth, development, must be an incremental learning process. Under this dogma the adultocentric picture of the infant and of incremental learning is the only one conceivable: What else could learning in infants be like? So, as I said, in important ways, infants must already be little adults in order to be able to grow into adults. Within a smooth, incremental model of learning there is no room for truly qualitative change – by assumption. There can be no change in kind during the course of development. QED: by retroactive reasoning, the infant is the competent infant (that is, assuming that the adult is the competent adult). Let us remember these dogmas later when we come to discuss the infant's madness.

What can be said about this view of infancy? For our purposes, its obvious and most important consequence is that its application virtually guarantees that one's conception of first language learning, too, will be in terms of one or another version of incremental learning theory.[35] In an environment that sees incremental learning theories as the preferable option, the child's linguistic competence is almost sure to be seen as progressing logically, moving in a relatively orderly progression from babbling to words to sentences, from primitive to sophisticated use of grammar, from simple to complex definitions and meanings, and so on. (And it must have had an adult-like foundation, such as Noam Chomsky's universal Language Acquisition Device, or its successor conception, Universal Grammar.) As Taylor points out, an important corollary is that, in principle, the way in which incremental learning theory or the traditional kinds of genetic theory are used to explain and formalize first language acquisition is much the same as the way in which all manner of learning in non-human animals is explained and theorized about. In its most tortured form, this theory is used to validate the popular belief that the 'language' acquired by higher animals such as chimpanzees is essentially much like human language and is acquired in much the same way.[36] Incremental theory also grounds models of later language learning in older children and adults (including learning a second language), but in these applications that type of theory is more defensible and useful, especially outside philosophy.[37] Once the child has an adequate linguistic foundation, explaining further language learning ostensively (at least in part) is no longer question-begging – but the paradox of the ground remains.

The ineffable infant and genetic theories

[handwritten: Charles Taylor]

I have said that unlike the smooth progression posited by incremental learning theories, true genetic theories of learning postulate relatively abrupt, quasi-step-wise qualitative changes – changes in ontology. With respect to language acquisition, Taylor calls the infant's first, most momentous of these discontinuous kinds of steps 'entering the linguistic dimension'. He says that prior to this entry, the infant is essentially in the same situation as any other non-speaking animal. At this stage of development, instrumental-incremental learning theories may well be useful and appropriate in academic or clinical contexts.[38] At any rate, all that we can know about the nature of the infant's experience must be inferred from external observations, and all that we can see is that the infant responds behaviorally to signs and signals, just like rats in a maze, or Pavlov's dogs. All other inferences about what goes on in the infant are necessarily guesses.

I want to emphasize that claiming that all that we can know about what goes on in infants is like what goes on in non-human animals means just that and only that: that is all that we can know about the infants' (and the animals') experiences. This position does not deny (or confirm) that something is going on 'inside' the infant, that it is 'experiencing'. Almost certainly, something is going on, but, equally certainly, something is also going on in other animals. The position that I am promulgating only insists that whatever it is that is going on in the infant, we cannot (or at least should not) say what it is – but also that as Wittgenstein says about pain, while it is not a 'something', neither is it a 'nothing'.[39] If we refrain from guessing, that is all we can say about infant experiencing. We cannot even imagine what it might be, unless we anthropomorphize. Of course, we are free to make guesses – for instance, claim that anyone can see that the infant is 'thinking' or 'planning' or 'hungry' – but I insist that any such formulation we make, any description we offer of what is going on in the infant, necessarily can be no better than a guess, an extension of the kinds of inference that we make about what is going on in adults on the basis of their non-verbal behavior and our experience of ourselves, our 'inner life'. Some may maintain that such guesses abut the experiences of infants are not guesses at all, that our interpretations of the child's manifest behaviors are obviously true and accurate. That, however, remains an intuitively grounded presupposition – and ought to be identified as such. Others may regard questioning the standard beliefs as ridiculous (a baby cries in a certain way; it is in pain; in another way, it is hungry), but these remain guesses, nevertheless. We do not have access to the child's inner life (and contrary to the claims of many, neither does, or ever can, neuroscience).[40] One can insist that anyone, any fool, can see that the child is, say, angry, or anxious, or happy, but that is circular reasoning: we know a child's inner life is much like an adult's because we have assumed that similar expressions or behaviors must mean the same in the infant. Elsewhere I have argued at length that the neonate state is ineffable, must remain so, and that leaving it at that – essentially, accepting a *via negativa* definition of early infant experience – can offer significant advantages in certain contexts.[41]

Under a genetic theory of learning, the child's way of being in the world changes drastically and mysteriously when it dramatically and quickly 'enters the linguistic dimension', as Taylor puts it, when it moves beyond the signal-responding stage. Although it is but one of the many discontinuities that characterize maturation, this change may well be the most momentous. In Taylor's perspective and terminology, in contrast with other animals, the child now begins to become disengaged from the tightly coupled stimulus-and-response world. It is able to step back, start to reflect, abstract, classify, self-refer, define, mean – to 'double the text' – a momentous move indeed. As Guignon puts it,

> Although animals and prelinguistic infants can busy themselves with tools, the complexity of the full human capacity for undertaking to act is impossible for them. Their activities do not participate in *our* 'world' – where this term is used in a Heideggerian sense that implies a weave of contrasts among more or less explicitly formulated self-interpretations and evaluations. Animals and infants have not mastered the articulate structure of roles and goals – of norms, standards, and conventions – that make up our involvement in the human world. If this is the cases, however, then we should

also recognize that there are limits to the degree to which we can ascribe our peculiarly human mental language to nonlinguistic and prelinguistic creatures.[42] 1583

After stepping into the linguistic dimension, the child begins to live in a world of symbols, of reading and writing. It increasingly becomes distanced from a simple, unitary, amorphous, ineffable, unreflective 'being in the world', an unthematized attunement to nature. Inexplicably, the child now begins to 'have' expressive language, to somehow have acquired the background understanding that is needed for understanding ostension. It begins to have that which Herder identified as being left unexplained in Condillac's circular explanation of language acquisition:

> The sentence 'The book is on the table' designates a book and a table in a certain relation; but it can be said to express my thought, or my perception, or my belief that the book is on the table... What is meant by 'expression' here? I think it means roughly this: something is expressed, when it is embodied in such a way as to be made manifest.[43]

Of course, even after the child has taken this step and thus has begun to ingest the default view of language (at least in our culture), it still will be sometime before they become aware of the various elements contained in that received view, and able to articulate them. (This will become an important point later on.) That is, at first, for some time after stepping into the language dimension, the concept of a word, sentence, of reference could not be explicitly articulated by the child. They just start to talk – a dramatic change from the babbling stage, but inexplicable to both the infant and their caregivers. They are not yet able to make abstract statements such as 'language is made up of words according to rules'. The qualitative change just happens, and very quickly at that. Adults begin to correct grammar, offer definitions, use language referentially. In the first stages of the infant's step into the language dimension, the 'knowledge' they have acquired about language by this inexplicable step is still primal, close to Michael Polanyi's notorious and paradoxical concept of tacit knowledge:

> Now we see tacit knowledge opposed to explicit knowledge; but these two are not sharply divided. While tacit knowledge can be possessed by itself, explicit knowledge must rely on being tacitly understood and applied. Hence all knowledge is either tacit or rooted in tact knowledge. A wholly explicit knowledge is unthinkable... [Yet

paradoxically] while it is true that all explicit knowledge rests on tacit knowledge, we would have no concept of the tacit without the explicit.[44]

Taylor says that the idea of entering the linguistic dimension 'gives us a picture of language as making possible new purposes, new levels of behavior, new meanings, and hence it is not explicable within a framework of human life conceived without language'[45] – as I read it: within a mathematical-logical framework – the state process formalism-dominated view. The questions that (true) genetic theories raise

> are all difficult and deep. I mean by that latter term not only that they touch fundamental questions about ourselves, but that they are baffling and very difficult to formulate, let alone find a clear strategy to investigate... We are not clear yet, certainly not agreed, on what to make of them.[46]   *Taylor*

I doubt that we ever will know.

What conceptions of infancy, language acquisition, language and worldview are associated with genetic theories of learning? As I see it, all that these can tell us about the infant's experiences and also about the step into the linguistic dimension is basically negative. Genetic theories automatically tell us that the competent infant model ought to be jettisoned, but they don't prescribe an alternative. In that sense, genetic learning theories are only restrictive; they rule out what has become a large and familiar territory. Thus, the first consequence of adopting genetic theories of learning and expressive conceptions of language is that they leave us very much at sea. They take away answers – but that is the very kind of a start that I believe to be necessary, almost by definition, if we want to move toward a previously unthought way of conceptualizing our world threats. It becomes obvious that the first step needs to be a removal. Leaving the usual options behind is what forces us to look elsewhere. In the present case, we need to look for an alternative to the competent infant conception. (We can begin to see the possible relevance of all this talk about babies to the principal problem we are addressing: humanity's perilous state.)

Psychodynamic models of infancy

Considerable thought about individual human development can be found in Freud's explorations, and in more than a century of subsequent worldwide clinical work and thought by his many successors. There is the perpetual question about the scientific status of this corpus, about the legitimacy of its theories. That is a very long story, and I don't intend to go into it here. (I have done so in a number of contexts in numerous publications.)[47] I submit that this is a non-issue here because we want to leave familiar sanctioned scientific, dualist models and theories behind and explore other, radical alternatives.

Freud was determined to get psychoanalysis accepted as a legitimate, respectable science and he never tried of claiming to do science. What is important for us is that he may have been conventionally ontoepistemological in many ways – but not in all. For example, in *Civilization and its Discontents* he raises the possibility that the neonate does not live in a dualistic world, that instead the infant is not yet able to distinguish between self and other, inside and outside world, that these kinds of distinction develop only later. The idea here is that originally, at birth, the child has only what Freud called a 'primary ego-feeling' – an oceanic feeling, a feeling of limitlessness, unbounded; all is self (or, equivalently, other). At one stage of his work, Freud was neutral about that idea. At any rate, he likened the oceanic feeling to being in love, when 'the boundary between ego and object [self and other] threaten to melt away '. Other than in infants and lovers, he considers such a state 'in which boundary lines between ego and the external world become uncertain or in which they are actually drawn incorrectly' to be highly pathological.[48] For Freud, psychological health requires clear boundaries to exist and be maintained between one's ego and the external world. There need to be 'clear and sharp lines of demarcation'.[49]

Freud does entertain the possibility that at first the infant is in a non-dual or unitary state, that it begins to differentiate between 'self' and 'world' only gradually. This differentiation leads to the child's increasing appreciation of what Freud called the 'reality principle'. That is, the shift from the initial unitary to the 'healthy' dualist state can be conceptualized as a movement toward healthy 'reality testing' – the ability to accurately (that is, 'realistically') differentiate between excitations that are coming in from the outside world from those originating in the organism's own internal world (ideas, emotions, fantasies, pains):

An infant at the breast does not as yet distinguish his ego from the external world as the source of the sensations flowing in upon him. He gradually learns to do so, in response to various promptings. He must be very strongly impressed by the fact that some sources of excitation ... can provide him with sensations at any moment, whereas other sources evade him from time to time – among them what he desires most of all, his mother's breast – and only reappear as a result of his screaming for help. In this way there is for the first time set over against the ego an 'object', in the form of something which exists 'outside' and which is only forced to appear by a special action... In this way the ego detaches itself from the world. Or, to put it more correctly, originally the ego includes everything, later it separates off an external world from itself. Our present [mature] ego-feeling is, therefore, only a shrunken residue of a much more inclusive – indeed, an all-embracing – feeling which corresponded to a more intimate bond between the ego and the world around it.[50]

A later major figure in the psychoanalytic world, Hans Loewald, believes that "the infant spends most of his day in a half-sleeping, half-waking state... the infant is only one global structure, one fleeting and very perishable mental entity that [is] neither ego nor object, neither a self nor another."[51] Yet another analyst, the controversial Jacques Lacan, believes that

One cannot even say that a child *knows* what it wants prior to the assimilation of language: when a baby cries, the *meaning* of that act is provided by the parents or caretakers who attempt to name the pain the child seems to be expressing (e.g., 'she must be hungry'). There is perhaps a sort of general discomfort, coldness, or pain, but its meaning is imposed, as it were, by the way in which it is interpreted by the child's parents.[52]

It is vitally important to recognize that this first unitary (non-dual) postnatal situation is unimaginable to us, saturated as we are in Cartesian dualisms and adult language. As adumbrated in Chapter 1, what this merger hypothesis posits is the most radical departure imaginable from the hegemonic dualism that Richard Rorty labeled the Cartesian–Lockean–Kantian (CLK) tradition[53] – a pattern that famously bristles with incoherence, paradox and fatally reductionistic thought,[54] yet continues to dominate our worldview. Actually, this dualism has an even older ancestry,[55] and so the radical hypothesis concerning the unitary neonate's state challenges more than just the modern CLK dualist tradition. At any rate, not only must we admit that we cannot conceptualize this ineffable state, but also we need to find ways of taking advantage of the *via negativa* to which the posit of ineffability leads us. In an earlier work I began to show the advantages of doing so.[56]

Furthermore, Freud also considers the radical possibility that the impact (aspects) of this undifferentiated start may extend into adulthood:

> If we may assume that there are many people in whose mental life this primary ego-feeling has persisted to a greater of less degree, it would exist in them side by side with the narrower and more sharply demarcated ego-feeling of maturity, like a kind of counterpart to it...[as] a feeling of an indissoluble bond, of being one with the external world as a whole. But we have a right to assume the survival of something that was originally there, alongside of what was later derived from it? Undoubtedly... [W]hat is primitive is commonly preserved alongside of the transformed version which has arisen from it.[57] *C & Discontent*

To me, at this stage, Freud's thinking implicitly reflects a remarkable (though not very successful) attempt to integrate genetic and incremental conceptions of learning: the posited initial state is *sui generis*, unitary, and the successor state is a change in kind; reality testing is a new ability. That is the genetic learning phase of this model of ontogenesis. When the successor state becomes dominant, it continues to evolve along dualistic conventional lines into adulthood 'gradually', incrementally (although Freud and his successors do posit some further discontinuities). That is the long, mostly incremental, phase. I believe that this is yet another expression of Freud's ambivalence about the earliest childhood stages. He says that 'From my own experience I could not convince myself of the primary nature of such a feeling'; yet he adds: 'but this gives me no right to deny that it [the oceanic feeling] does in fact occur in other people.'[58] Loewald remarked that Freud

> confesses his unwillingness to plunge into the depths of primordial, buried psychological levels of the primary narcissistic or related stages, and investigate them... Among the reasons for not doing so are his theoretical bias in favor of a biological instinct concept, and his reluctance, amounting to an aversion, to involve himself deeply in the investigation of mental stages and states where the subject-object polarity does not [yet] hold.[59]

Freud's focus remained militantly on the Oedipus complex, a much later event than the child's move out of the unitary state. He treated the earlier eras and issues only cursorily, almost schematically.

There is still no consensus among psychodynamically oriented thinkers and practitioners about the nature of the earliest childhood state, although there is no shortage of theorizing. According to the perspective that I am developing, there can be no resolution; the theorizing is suspect – as I see it, it mostly reflects efforts to be scientifically respectable. An extreme currently held minority position that may be the radical, difficult-to-believe exception is the view of ontogenesis promulgated by the disciplined, very well-trained but entirely unorthodox psychiatrist and analyst Stanislav Grof. His so-called holotropic work challenges and undermines the most basic metaphysical assumptions of Western science. From decades of careful clinical work he has concluded that because it limits its thinking about ontogenesis to post-natal biography, the usual psychiatric, psychoanalytic and allied clinical thought is drastically incomplete and impoverished. Grof has expanded what he calls 'the cartography of the human psyche' to include '*the perinatal domain*, related to the trauma of biological birth, and *the transpersonal domain*, which accounts for such phenomena as experiential identification with other people, animals, plants, and other aspects of nature'.[60] I realize that on first exposure his approach and position are almost certain to strike one as absurd and fanciful. However, his extensive work spans decades and is carefully documented, closely argued and supported by a great deal of clinical experience that is reported in considerable detail. Even though its framework, claims and results go against virtually everything we think we know clinically and commonsensically about human development and, for that matter, about our world, I find Grof's work convincing and compelling, certainly most interesting and deserving careful study.[61] At any rate, I mention it here primarily to illustrate the breadth of unconventional thinking about early development that a psychodynamically informed framework can allow and support. Grof's work will play no further role in what follows.

Hatching and maturity

The different perspective that I will explore begins with the premise that for some months after biological birth, what goes on in the infant is ineffable. There are few theories of infancy that make this assumption. One of these is Margaret Mahler's early version of her so-called separation-individuation model of infant development. She was an important figure in mid-twentieth-century psychoanalysis who together with Manuel Fuhrer founded the Masters Childrens Center in Manhattan.

There she did extensive clinical work and conducted observational studies that led her to the separation-individuation hypothesis.

According to Mahler's earlier thought, an ineffable initial post-natal situation evolves into the beginnings of our familiar adult-like way via an equally ineffable step that she calls 'hatching', or 'the psychological birth of the human infant': the inscrutable process that takes the undifferentiated infant into rudimentary forms of the adult's way of being in the world. (I see hatching as very much like Taylor's radical step into the linguistic dimension.) Here is her brief description of the process:

> The biological birth of the human infant and the psychological birth of the individual are not coincident in time. The former is a dramatic, observable, and well-circumscribed event; the latter a slowly unfolding intrapsychic process.[62] For the more or less normal adult, the experience of himself as both fully 'in,' and fully separate from, the 'world out there' is taken for granted as a given of life... But this, too, is the result of a slowly unfolding process... Like any intrapsychic process, this one reverberates throughout the life cycle. It is never finished; it remains always active; new phases of the life cycle see new derivatives of the earliest processes still at work.[63]

(Later she backed away from this unitary view of earliest infancy and adopted a more conventional, scientifically acceptable hypothesis regarding the nature of the newborn's experiencing.)

Obviously, from the perspective of incremental learning theorizing, this conception of the state of the newborn is simply unacceptable. As already noted, conventional wisdom, cognitive behavioral and other sanctioned approaches such as structural ones demand and insist that a child's developing 'mental capacities' – language, cognition, perception, intentionality, affect – must already be there at birth in some form (the competent infant), that such competencies cannot appear *ex nihilo*, that Leibniz's principle of reason must always hold. But I also have argued that as long as one does insist on that position, then one is also doomed to remain trapped within Cartesian thinking, to retain the conventional metaphysics that Heidegger idiosyncratically calls 'subjectivism'. I would ask: Why is Leibniz's principle unchallengeable, sacred? Isn't it just a pronouncement supported by commonsense? Isn't its justification self-referential, circular? As I have said before, if one wants to be able to envision a truly alternative view of self and world (and thus perhaps also a more productive view of our current predicaments), then one has to move outside the frameworks of incremental learning theories, competent infants, received view of language, dichotomized ontologies. That is why I chose to use Mahler's model, with its generative notion of hatching, as the basis for looking at first language acquisition.

Under Mahler's model, all adult beliefs and perceptions about ourselves and our world (and our language) come to be seen as second-order phenomena, and, in that sense, artifacts whose ancestry is unimaginable. That is, they are derivative, contingent, arising in unknowable ways (hatching, the infant's psychological birth, its entry into the linguistic dimension) out of an unknowable ground. These adult views and ways of being in the world rest on an undefinable foundation, and in this sense are illusory, ungrounded. One can conceptualize them as precipitants or sedimentations that have condensed out of an unimaginable, unstructured, formless, primal unitary source. Under this non- or anti-vision of the earliest state, language, perception, boundaries, individuated objects, cognition, thought, concepts – everything and anything that we see as part of self and world – differentiate out of something unknown and unknowable, unimaginable, alien. From this perspective, language is not an autonomous entity but just one aspect, although probably the most momentous one, of a connected network that we as post-hatched beings have come to see as a variety of discrete, articulated experiences and abilities – the precipitates referred to above. Indeed, it becomes questionable whether one can legitimately think about this network in terms of independent components at all.

This strange conception bears repeating: language, along with everything else in the constellation of our experience of self and world, is neither a nothing nor a something. From a murky, amorphous paradoxical ground, phenomena do emerge and begin to congeal into a languaged self that exists in a world that included that self. Wittgenstein sensed this: 'When we first begin to believe anything, what we believe is not a single proposition, it is a whole system of propositions. (Light dawns gradually over the whole),'[64] This kind of emerging but fluid vision is also reminiscent of Heidegger's writing about the clearing, about revealing and withdrawing. Indeed, as the philosopher Lee Braver has pointed out, these 'two great philosophers passed each other in mid-career',[65] at one time converging on what Braver has called the idea of 'groundless grounds' – perhaps another term for the neonate's ineffable being.[66]

It seems reasonable to assume, further, that since all of these apparently discrete aspects of adult experience and being once were an amorphous singularity, in some way they remain interconnected throughout life (as Freud hinted might be the case). Under this assumption, all of our normal, dualistic, cognitive ways of understanding ourselves as individuals in an external world of objects and events come to be seen as insistent, persistent distortions riding on top of an unimaginable originary situation: the neonate's unimaginably fluid, unboundaried, non-languaged initial non-experience. In many cases one can safely ignore this unsettling underpinning and proceed on the basis of our standard illusions (we call these commonsense, or science). However, I believe that in many other situations one invites trouble by doing so, by seeing and dealing with fragmentation and individuation where actually there continues to be an underlying unity, connectedness. For example, we have quantum theory's inexplicable, mind-boggling phenomenon of non-locality, or relativity's four-dimensional space–time continuum (but these still do retain the Cartesian dualism – after all, there has to be an observer, and data). The trouble is, it is not always easy to tell in a particular situation whether it is appropriate or harmless to operate on the basis of our normal commonsense assumptions (illusions) about world and self, or whether so doing would exact heavy costs. For example, I have become convinced that operating under the assumptions of the received view of language and the concomitant views of self and world is not desirable in serious psychotherapy. The costs may be hidden but, as I see it, they are heavy nevertheless. But one must admit that the paradoxes that are there but well concealed in the conventional Cartesian world (or even in the world of contemporary physics) become explicit and highly troublesome as soon as one begins to search for a genuine alternative.

In short, according to this picture, and as some Eastern thinkers and other sages have been trying to tell us for millennia, our taken-for-granted world beliefs and perceptions necessarily float on quicksand – which, incidentally, can account for the infinitely many paradoxes and dead ends of the perennial disputes about realism and antirealism, about the nature of self and world, that have hounded Western thought for millennia.[67] The sages have already told us that what we experience as apparently autonomous, separate things and experiences, ourselves included, actually is unitary.[68] I return to this view later, in the context of humanity's madness.

Choosing an infant model

If the competent infant view of early infancy is so widely and uncritically accepted, presumably empirically supported by an overwhelming number of credible scientific observations that study this or that manifestation of the infant's competence, then what could be wrong? How could I challenge these concepts and findings? To me, these are strange questions. I have already hinted at the answer but would like to elaborate.

The underlying conceptual weaknesses of the hypothesis and its investigations seem so painfully obvious, but apparently they aren't. In fact, I have tried to point them out during numerous contentious discussions with traditional researchers and academicians working in the field of infant cognition and behavior who championed this competent infant model. All too often the traditionalists could not understand either my objections nor my envisioned alternative. This exactly duplicates Herder's experience with Condillac, as discussed by Taylor. Let us remind ourselves that, in Taylor's words, Condillac, Herder's opponent,

> was unaware that he had left anything out. He wouldn't have known where Herder was 'coming from,' just as his heirs today, the proponents of chimp language, talking commuters, and truth-conditional theories of meaning, find the analogous objections to their views gratuitous and puzzling.[69]

What Condillac couldn't see, and what 'his heirs today' still can't see, is the question-begging nature of this conception of infant learning of language, that it presupposes what it claims to discover and confirm. I am pretty sure that I understand the point of view of the champions of the competent infant model.[70] It is not complex and not difficult to comprehend. My sense is that the model's fervent espousers cannot comprehend my perspective. It draws on ways of thinking (especially Heidegger's and Wittgenstein's) that are unfamiliar and baffling, or only superficially understood, and consequently often regarded as nonsensical.

The same kind of circularity that flaws positions such as Condillac's also flaws the arguments of the expounders of the competent infant hypothesis. That ought not to be difficult to see, as I began to discuss earlier. There are basic logical weaknesses in the scientific evidence offered in support of the competent infant conception. Consider what the nature of that evidence could possibly be – or better still, what it could not possibly be: the competent infant's own report of its experience. The observed data can be just about anything else available to an external observer – visible, audible or any other kinds of perceived signals or cues, neurobiological data included. These must then be put in a context, interpreted (framed in language and a theory), fitted to a preconceived hypothetical formal system and so on. The issue is one's taking something non-verbal and externally observed, and claiming that its interpretation is a report of 'objective fact', claiming that one is veridically reporting observations that are telling us about 'inner' experiencing when in fact one is making interpretations – interpretations that are soaked in the received view, at that.

Now, if one were engaged in some more or less standard, even mundane, investigation – say, a pediatrician trying to find out why an infant is constantly crying, or a mother trying to decide whether it is time to feed an infant – then use of this normal science's framework and methodology of hypothesized theory, standard data-gathering, processing and interpretation (less charitably, the use of commonsense) would be quite appropriate and adequate. That is being done all of the time, and most of the time probably quite successfully. But that is not what we are trying to do here. We are not examining the neonatal state in order to discover some additional detail to add to what we already know and can quantify, formalize – like the infant's current weight, attention span or clinical status. Nor are we preparing a paper for publication in a mainstream research journal. Here we are attempting to unearth fundamentals about the child's experiences during the early weeks of postnatal life. If then we simply act on preconceptions, on the adultocentric dogma that any neonate is a competent infant; that a certain facial grimace is essentially much like an adult's smile and means essentially the same thing; that looking away from a stimulus means that the child 'is bored'; that emitting a certain kind of cry means that the child is 'in pain' or 'experiencing discomfort'; that reacting to various configurations of objects in certain ways is essentially the same thing as doing rudimentary arithmetic; that a certain neurological brain activity means the same thing as does its adult counterpart;[71] and on and on – then inevitably, necessarily, we will seem to have obtained yet further support for the picture of the competent infant, the proto-adult who obviously evolves via incremental learning into the standard (competent?) adult. The nature of our findings will be preordained. We will find that which we have put in place. And that is what is wrong with the whole picture: the fallacious weakness, the circularity that for some, to me, inexplicable reason cannot be perceived or understood by the fervent proponents of the standard hypothesis who find experimental support for their competent infant hypothesis – which really is a preconception. I am repeating Herder's objection in a contemporary garb.

The problem of scientific infant observation and study is very much like the problem that one faces when one is trying to scientifically explore the inner workings and experiences of non-human animals – when one is trying to establish 'what it is like to be a bat'. It is the problem of studying language-less thought, a problem that has been raised with respect to humans as well as other higher animals, such as chimpanzees.[72] As I see it, it is a thankless enterprise if one expects to find out something truly new. Take, for example, José Luis Bermúdez's recent *Thinking Without Words*,[73] a book that seems to have received some acclaim. It claims to provide 'a challenging new theory of the nature of non-linguistic thought' that illuminates the highly problematic question of how complex cognitive behaviors that seem rational can possibly be performed by non-linguistic creatures (animals, infants). It is a theory that explains what such an apparently cognitive but language-less process would be like: 'Bermúdez offers a conceptual framework for treating human infants and non-human animals as genuine thinkers.'[74] Expectably, the author, a dedicated cognitivist, addresses the issue entirely within a scientific-rational-objectifying, dichotomous, respectably logical framework. Given what I have said, I do not believe that he could possibly find a way of explaining 'thought without words' other than in terms of a symbolic, formalistic, logico-scientific model – a method that is bound to keep him within the standard ontological-epistemological, depersonalized, separatist, reductive framework of science. And indeed we find that Bermúdez cannot deliver, cannot reach his goal. So what does he do instead? He shifts his focus, recasts the issue and ends up saying in several places that his aim really is to gain 'insight' into apparently thought-based but language-less behaviors via formal-logical modeling. Well, providing an insight into wordless thought via a familiar analogy – some logico-mathematical or psychological model – is hardly a new kind of explanation, and indeed Bermúdez grants that this mode of explanation does not mean gaining any new understanding of 'what it is like' to be a non-linguistic creature that exhibits apparently reason-based behavior. He concludes that 'the fact of the matter...is that we have little idea of what the vehicle of nonlinguistic thought might be'.[75] To me, this admission still implies that we have some idea, but, as I see it, works such as his do not and cannot give us any idea, little or not, of 'what it would be like to be a bat'. I maintain that the entire field of consciousness studies, Bermúdez's effort included, gives us no idea at all, sheds absolutely no new light on, 'what it is to be like' a non-linguistic yet presumably thinking creature.[76] His book, like others, at best only gives the illusion of having done so, as it necessarily must. Ascribing thought to non-linguistic, non-speaking organisms, to bats and babies, may be all right for pet owners and adoring parents, but this practice is neither acceptable nor defensible in serious, presumably scientific, studies that purport to investigate the inner experiences of 'non-linguistic and prelinguistic creatures' – or for that matter, in any serious studies of human consciousness.[77] I will return to the subject of experiencing in Chapter 4.

We do have two options for how we can conceptualize the neonate – as a competent infant or an ineffable infant. Neither can be validated. Therefore in any given situation the model that we choose to employ is partly a matter of personal preference, of dogmatic allegiance, but what is or should be most important is our reason for asking the question, why we want to know, what the purposes of our investigation are. Thus it is not a matter of which model is right, true, correct because, as I have argued, the question is unresolvable in principle. So it is the aim of a study that is crucial to model choice. It is one thing if we are owners trying to decide how to deal with our pet, or a dedicated cognitive behaviorist trying to get a paper published. It is quite another matter if we are trying to unconventionally reconceptualize the world's dire state in order to improve our understanding via fundamental re-examinations of our presuppositions, by reconsidering the complex and limiting language-and-worldview constellation that grounds our remedial efforts, as it does everything else.

In Chapter 4, I begin to explore the nature of humanity's other momentous developmental moment, this time an analogous phylogenetic developmental step: humanity's acquisition of literacy, its step into the world of reading and writing.

4
Literacy and Primary Orality

In some ways the maturational step that we begin to consider in this chapter is similar to the neonate's entry into the linguistic dimension. It, too, has far-reaching implications; is mostly ignored or else misunderstood and trivialized; has ineffable roots; and, as we shall see, it, too, contributes to humanity's madness. It is the phylogenetic step into reading and writing, humankind's acquisition of literacy. Overall, both changes obviously have something to do with acquiring a new language-related ability. We will see that these two very different, apparently independent, developmental landmark events have become intertwined and related because of the complex, synergistic roles that they play in the generation and maintenance of humankind's madness. To understand these connections will require further preparatory work, so for the time being we will focus on the nature of literacy and its predecessor as much as possible, letting the issues pertaining to individuals' acquisition of language remain in the background.

Scholars have written and debated a good deal about the evolution of literacy. They have traced it from obscure beginnings in various pre-alphabetical symbolic notational systems through the early stages of writing as we now know it, to the various later technological developments ranging from the invention of printing to word-processing, texting and cell phones. Reading and writing were

> a very late development in human history. The first script...was developed...less than 6000 years ago. The alphabet, which was invented only once, so that every alphabet in the world derives directly or indirectly from the original Semitic alphabet, came into existence only around 1500 BC. Speech is ancient, archaic. Writing is brand-new.[1]

Thus a very long non-literate period preceded the emergence of reading and writing. There were eons during which humanity could not have had any inkling that there could be such a thing as literacy.

Primary or pristine orality

The linguist Walter Ong calls the state that preceded humanity's entry into literacy 'primary' or 'pristine orality' (hereafter 'p-orality'). Although the idea of such a state seems straightforward, p-orality is not an easy, simple concept. Most literary scholars, linguists, psychologists and philosophers who study the development of literacy have shied away from studying this condition or even speculating about it, for a number of good reasons. By definition, textual data from p-oral times cannot exist, so there can only be some indirect evidence about the p-oral way of life. Scholarly inferences or hypotheses about it must necessarily be highly speculative, based on non-textual artifacts of some kind, and/or on clues and cues culled from later eras' text fragments. Some speculations may be more convincing or commonsensical than others, but they still are, and must remain, speculation.

We have here a situation strikingly analogous to the neonatal state. Our knowledge about p-orality is just as innately limited as our knowledge about the infant's initial way of being in the world. About the only aspect of p-orality of which we can be reasonably sure is that its dominant sensory modality would have been aural-oral. Without writing, languaging must have been almost entirely an acoustic affair. (I believe we can ignore the remote possibility that p-orals had a sign language. They may have had some rudimentary signaling systems, but the invention and development of any but the most primitive version of signing seems almost impossible in a non-literate culture. Signing is modeled on writing.)

The study of p-orality, then, is necessarily beset by innate difficulties. If scholars nevertheless wanted to tackle the state, they would have to work at its edges, so to speak. The work of Eric Havelock, a major scholar who investigated the literacy/orality doublet in several contexts, is typical in that regard. Speaking about one of his own important monographs, he comments that 'The intention of this book is to present a unified picture of a crisis that occurred in the history of human communication, when Greek orality transformed itself into Greek literacy.'[2] The Greek orality to which he refers is the orality of the age of Plato and Homer, an age when orality – no longer p-orality – had of course coexisted with reading and writing for a number of millennia. His study, then, clearly is not a study of the p-oral state, and the relevance of his findings to life under that state must remain speculative and tentative. Havelock simply stays away from saying anything about the true primal precursor of Greek literacy, the p-oral era. He studies one of p-orality's temporal neighbors instead, and a rather distant neighbor at that if the estimates about the dates of humanity's entry into literacy are even close to accurate. We will see that Havelock was acutely aware of the inescapable conceptual and practical problems that are raised by any attempt to study p-orality, so his evasive policy, to study traces left from the Greek era, makes good sense.

Walter Ong, a linguist who was strongly influenced by Havelock and who, as I mentioned, coined and defined the term 'primary' or 'pristine orality', was one of the few important scholars who in spite of these insurmountable research obstacles wrote and speculated a good deal about this long and veiled enigmatic precursor of the literate way of being in the world. He, like Havelock, began his work by studying eras during which literacy had already existed for millennia. He began as 'an expert in the history of the Renaissance'[3] and he explored linguistic questions rooted 'deep in Renaissance and earlier intellectual history'[4] – a very long distance from p-oral times. He first focused on orality-textuality issues in literate cultures, and only later extended his findings, drawing all sorts of inferences (making all sorts of guesses) about the condition of p-orality from studies of literate cultures. His work was widely admired, but he also was criticized for offering speculative, inadequately supported fundamental hypotheses about p-orality – as we have seen, an unavoidable consequence of the nature of that era.

Ong concluded that life in the p-oral state had been drastically different from life in a literate culture, that the two psychologies were almost unimaginably different. His view was that the entry into literacy fundamentally changed people's way of being in the world. The Oxford linguist Roy Harris, among others, dismissed claims that a new kind of mentality arose with literacy. He pointed out that similar guesses had already been made in the eighteenth century,[5] that

> the important difference between before and after the advent of utilitarian literacy is not essentially a difference between typical ways of thinking about the world, of classifying and ordering, of overcoming memory limitation, or of strategies for acquiring knowledge, although all the differences doubtless correlate with the spread of writing... [What is] more fundamental... is a shift in conceptions of language itself.[6]

The cognitive developmental psychologist David Olson also rejected Ong's hypotheses about p-orality on the basis that we are all 'cognitively the same'.[7] Along the same lines, in their influential study, Scribner and Cole could not find any empirical verification for Ong's conjectures – hardly surprising, given the constraints inherent in the subject matter.[8]

At times, Ong insisted that p-orality as a way of being a self in the world must necessarily be almost unimaginable to us. We don't realize what becoming literate has done to humanity, and therefore cannot see what life without literacy would be like. He repeatedly cautioned that

> freeing ourselves of chirographic and topographic bias in our under-standing of language is probably more difficult than any of us can imagine... We – readers of books such as this – are so literate that it is very difficult for us to conceive of an oral universe of commu-nication or thought except as a variant of a literate universe... The purely oral tradition or primary orality is not easy to conceive of accurately and meaningfully. Writing makes 'words' appear similar to things because we think of words as the visible marks signaling words to decoders: we can see and touch such inscribed 'words' in texts and books... Fully literate persons can only with great difficulty imagine what a primary oral culture is like, that is, a culture with no knowledge whatsoever of writing or even of the possibility of writing. Try to imagine a culture where no one has ever 'looked up' anything. In a primary oral culture, the expression 'to look up' something' is an empty phrase: it would have no conceivable meaning. With-out writing, words as such have no visual presence, even when the objects they represent [NB!] are visual. They are sounds. You might 'call' them back – 'recall' them. But there is nowhere to 'look' for them. They have no focus and not trace (a visual metaphor, showing dependency on writing), not even a trajectory. They are occurrences, events.... Oral folk have no sense of a name as a tag, for they have no idea of a name as something that can be seen. Written or printed representations of words can be labels; real, spoken words cannot be.[9]

Ong did not always follow his own caveats, as we shall see.

Speculations about primary orality

At first glance the state of p-orality, the way of life before humanity's entry into literacy, does not seem all that mysterious or difficult to imagine. We are inclined to think that it must have been very much like the way of life experienced currently by illiterates, a state that we readily understand and can empathize with – or at least think we can. Superficially there seems to be no reason to think otherwise, to believe that there would be significant psychological or philosophical differences between p-orals and those in our own culture who are illiterate or nearly so. In other words, it is tempting to believe that since we are so familiar with illiteracy in our time, since understanding it seems to pose little if any conceptual difficulties, since overcoming it (learning to read and write) is a mundane, commonplace, unproblematic process, that it is valid to extend this easy understanding to p-orality.

It is inviting, too, to believe that contemporary studies of illiterates or near-illiterates can and do illuminate what life had been like in a p–oral culture – and, more than likely, that belief is entirely wrong. The ability to read and write is not the essence of the differences between p-orality and literacy, any more than having technological gadgets, flourishing scientific disciplines and so on is the essence of what Heidegger calls 'rational-technological-calculative thinking'.[10] The main reason we are unable to intuit what being p-oral was like is that we do not, cannot begin to, appreciate or comprehend the complex impact of literacy. Literacy along with its effects has been evolving and elaborating for millennia, and now its consequences are so much part of our everyday lives and meaningful history that there is no way we could recognize any but the most obvious of its effects. The consequences that remain out of sight impact contemporary illiterates or near illiterates just as much as they do people who can read and write, and, in any case, according to Ong's own criteria, illiterates do not qualify as p-orals. (They know all about the possibility of literacy.)

Primary orality's ineffability

Let us take a closer look at the difficulties that confront scholars who want to study p-orality. Ong's colleague Eric Havelock has some illuminating things to say about the problem:

> Aside from the paradox by which language has to be used to understand language, that is, to understand itself, we face a comparable dilemma when we undertake to understand orality [I assume that Havelock is referring to p-orality]. For the chief source material provided for inspection is textual. How can a knowledge of orality be derived from its opposite? And even supposing texts can supply some sort of image of orality, how can that image be adequately

verbalized in a textural description of it, which presumably employs a vocabulary and syntax proper to textualization, not orality?

The same problem of contamination by literate idiom lurks behind the reporting by anthropologists and ethnologists of the stories and songs of the 'primitives' they studied in America, north and south, and in Polynesia. These inevitably suffer some manipulative interpretation which may (though not invariably) recast the native idiom in order to extract its 'meaning' for the modern mind... There always remains an insurmountable barrier to the understanding of orality.[11]

Havelock makes some telling arguments here, but the first, most blatant and also unavoidable impediment is that there simply are no more societies that qualify as being p-oral under Ong's stated criteria.

Second, could one validly substitute the study of what we might think are near-p-oral groups, our contemporary illiterates, or 'primitive' cultures living in remote areas? I have already argued against that possibility. Nevertheless, Ong draws some conclusions about p-orals from A. R. Luria's extensive fieldwork with illiterate as well as with somewhat literate persons, using Luria's research findings obtained in the remoter areas of Uzbekistan as an example of the nature of p-orality.[12] He also draws inferences from other similar studies, such as of the narrations of Navahoes telling Navaho folkloric animal stories.[13] In fact, he begins to refer to such groups as 'oral', further blurring and eroding the lines and sharp distinctions that he initially had posited.

The third point is quite straightforward. We cannot study p-orality directly, so scholars must resort to texts. Then, as Havelock put it, 'the chief source material provided for inspection is textual. How can a knowledge of orality be derived from its opposite?' It can't, without a great deal of hand-waving.

The fourth and last point is the problem of contamination, mentioned by Havelock and adumbrated above. It is closely related to the problems raised by studying near p-orals: even if a p-oral culture were still available for field study, there would be a fatal observer paradox – a matter that seems to come up repeatedly in a variety of contexts. Consider what current observation of truly p-oral culture would necessarily entail. It is almost certain that the scientific observer and the members of that culture would not speak the same language – at least not initially. It would be an unimaginable cosmic coincidence if they both happened to speak English, for example. Thus, one side or the other, or both, would have to learn another language. It takes but little reflection to realize just how much contamination, and how many tacit presuppositions, would be transferred during the course of this mutual learning process. P-orals would no longer be p-orals; they would be all too aware of literacy from the contact with their interlocutors.

The observer, too, is contaminated even before this mutual learning of languages has started. Dan Everett's study of the Pirahã, mentioned in Chapter 2, is a case in point. From an orthodox linguist's point of view, his most important finding was the Pirahã's lack of recursion (roughly, the nesting of clauses or sentences) in their syntax. When he analyzed the Pirahã's language, what struck him, what he could identify as anomalous, was the absence of recursion, a phenomenon that according to Noam Chomsky's theorizing is a universal feature of language. Everett could perceive this absence in the Pirahã language – or thought he could – and in his theoretical framework that would be a tremendously important finding. It would upset an important, prestigious dogma. At any rate, since he is a trained linguist, one of Everett's numerous givens about language would be that recursion had to be either present or absent in any language. Suppose, though, that in fact there had been something truly anomalous about recursion in the Pirahã language: suppose that their language in fact had been neither recursive nor non-recursive – like Wittgenstein's pain, not a something but not a nothing either, some third anomaly we might call 'a-recursion'.[14] That possibility is inconceivable to the mainstream linguist. Everett expresses no doubts about the presumption that recursion is a bivalent phenomenon. He doesn't find it necessary to even spell that out, so I don't see how he could possibly have recognized a third modality if there had in fact been one. This is one small example of the ways in which our thinking about p-orality are restricted by the observer's various kinds of constriction.

The problem introduced by language investigators' premises has been identified and thoroughly explored in a quite different context by Ian Robinson in an extended critique of Chomskean presuppositions in linguistics. He points out that while proponents of scientific investigations of language talk glibly about 'a complete collection of facts', one may well ask, 'how, in the absence of scientific as well as moral principle, one knows a fact when one sees it'.[15] He goes on to offer a Wittgenstein-like picture and questions. He imagines that a scientific investigator from an alien culture who is studying our language and culture comes upon two persons 'singing'. Robinson asks:

> How does he know that they are singing? And if, as may well be the case, he is genuinely doubtful, how will it be *proved* that they are

singing? By measuring their noises against some standard of musical time, melody, harmony, and the other things we like to think of as elements of music? The problem might just be that our persons are singing outside the criteria we have brought with us of what singing is.[16]

'How does he know they are singing in the first place?' The answer is that he 'knows' only by begging the question. He is making the same kind of mistake that Herder identified in Condillac's theorizing, or the same mistake made by the observers of the competent infant.

Literate humanity

Because of all of these considerations and weaknesses, I doubt whether Ong's speculative views of p-orality would be useful for my purposes. The doubts do keep me from using Ong's ideas about p-orality in what follows, although I will occasionally refer to some of his less problematic views. It is important for my purposes to keep open the question of what p-orality might be like. Eventually I, too, will speculate about it to help open up a space in which one can reconceptualize the received view of language, and, along with that, the framework that structures our (mis)perceptions of the dangers we face. For now we do not need any such conjectures. Rather, I want to focus on understanding literacy more deeply. In order to take advantage of some of Ong's insights about that state, about the only assumption about p-orals we need to make is one that seems evident – namely, that p-orals' lives were dominated by sound, that they lived in an aural/oral world. At this point I want to outline some characteristics of literate persons, in preparation for the upcoming explorations of humanity's madness. Unlike the features of p-orality, we *can* know the features of what life under literacy is like – at least to the degree that our preconceptions about it allow accurate perceptions.

Ong said that it was his desire to gain a better understanding of our own situation that motivated his study of the p-oral state in the first place. He believed that

A deeper understanding of pristine or primary orality enables us better to understand the new world of writing, what it truly is, and what functionally literate human beings really are: beings whose thought processes do not grow out of simply natural powers but our of these powers as structured, directly or indirectly, by the technology of writing. Without writing, the literate mind would not and could not think as it does, not only when engaged in writing but normally even when it is composing its thoughts in oral form. More than any other single invention, writing has transformed human consciousness.[17]

Although I am leery of using some of Ong's conception of the p-oral state, I have no reservations about using his views about the state of literacy. He gave that condition a great deal of thought, he was a prominent linguist, he could study literacy, so let us see what he had to say about it.

I take Ong's views mostly from two chapters of his pioneering *Orality and Literacy*: Chapter 3, 'Some psychodynamics of orality', and Chapter 4, 'Writing restructures consciousness'. Most of his conclusions about the p-oral and the literate states are inferred from the differences he ascribes to the two sensory modalities that he considers crucial and characteristic: vision and hearing. Basically, his views about the differences between p-orality and literacy hinge on his view that 'Sight isolates, sound incorporates.'[18] Sight dichotomizes, sound integrates and unifies. Ong begins his discussions by examining the characteristics of the experiences associated with these two perceptual/physical modalities. He discusses the evanescence of sound, its fleeting appearance and its temporal duration; that it cannot be blocked or captured; that it can be used to explore interiority (say, by tapping an object); that a produced sound can't be examined at leisure (certainly not by p-orals, not without technology), isn't a material object that can be captured and studied scientifically; that under p-orality, words are not conceptualized as labels since they lack materiality. Speaking unfolds over time (think of a story or song); once gone it is unrecoverable. Speech is difficult to remember, impossible to repeat exactly, or at least one can never be sure that one is doing so; speaking implies the presence of a listener; is difficult if not impossible to analyze formally without pinning it down by means of some notation or other 'writing' (say, recordings). Ong gives this example:

> If functionally literate persons are asked to think of the word 'nevertheless', they will all have present in imagination the letters of the word – vaguely perhaps, but unavoidably – in handwriting or typescript or print. If they are asked to think of the word 'nevertheless' for two minutes,120 seconds, without ever allowing any letters at all to enter their imaginations, they cannot comply. A person from a completely oral background of course has no such problem. He or she will

think only of the real word, a sequence of sounds, 'ne-ver-the-less'. For the real word 'nevertheless', the sounded word, cannot ever be present all at once, as written words deceptively seem to be. Sound exists only when it is going out of existence. By the time I get to the 'the-less', the 'ne-ver' is gone. To the extent that it makes all of a word appear present at once, writing falsifies.[19]

Note that Ong just assumes that p-orals 'think of the real *word*', just as literate people would – an example of his received view imposed assumption that language necessarily is atomic and made up of elements such as words being automatically applied. Who knows, who can ever know, whether p-orals actually thought of language as some thing, and, if so, whether they thought of 'it' as a thing composed of separate words that have separate referents and separate meanings, definitions? The possibility that they did not see language that way is exactly one of those options that would occur to literate observers only rarely if ever, especially if they were linguists, logicians, psychologists, philosophers, or scientists steeped in their scientific frameworks.

Via writing, language was able to become precisely just another of science's objects of study, a datum that can be acquired, and then analyzed at leisure. One major result of humankind's entering literacy is that is has led to our received view of language – the familiar formalized semiotic system – along with its ontoepistemological companion: our received view of 'self' and 'world', 'The Cartesian legacy [which] includes a conception of the world as consisting of minds and matter, a picture of truth as correct representation, and a belief that intelligibility is to be rooted in rationality.'[20]

Here is how one of Ong's editor's summarizes his views on writing:

Writing is not merely an exterior tool, but a practice that alters human consciousness to the degree to which it is, as Walter Ong says, 'interiorized'. Writing is 'interiorized' psychologically as the subject's experience is mediated to a significant degree by literate forms of discourse … Writing, proposes Ong, takes language out of the evanescent act of speaking and fixes oral utterance, an event in time, to written signs, objects in space. It thus removes language, and with it, thought, from an immediate personal, social, and cultural contingency. Such 'diaeresis' [roughly, segmentation] makes possible a progressive separation of knowledge from interpretation, of logic from rhetoric, of past record from present-day reconstruction, and of cumulative factual learning from the judgement and wisdom acquired by experience.[21]

Ong says that

> Functionally literate persons ... are not simply thinking and speaking human beings but chirographically thinking and speaking human beings .... The fact that we do not commonly feel the influence of writing on our thoughts shows that we have interiorized the technology of writing so deeply that without tremendous effort we cannot separate it from ourselves or even recognize its presence and influence.[22]

Many of the far-reaching and significant implications of this profound change are far from obvious. For example, under p-orality it almost surely would have been impossible to explain or interpret language, because, as Ong tells us, hermeneutics, interpretation of language, became possible only with the acquisition of writing:

> It is a commonplace that the formal study of hermeneutics or exegesis began by centering on texts ... Without writing, the literate mind would not and could not think as it does [there would be no 'literate mind'], and that is true not only when engaged in writing but even when it is composing its thoughts in oral form.[23]

Ong sees this change from orality to literacy reflected in a change in emotional climate. He argues that the dynamic, temporally dominated aural-oral world was mobile, warm, personally interactive, live, integrated with the living present, whereas the vision-dominated atemporal world of writing is cold, fixed, artificial, shallow, fragmented, reflexive, disengaged, constricted and constricting, estranging. In the present context, what I see as Ong's most important conclusion is that 'One of the most generalizable effects of writing is separation. Separation is also one of the most telling effects of writing ... It divides and distances, and it divides and distances all sorts of things in all sorts of ways.'[24] He anticipated my critique of the received view's separability assumption that was discussed in Chapter 2. He gives examples of this distancing, including the separation of known from knower, word from sound and existence, producer/originator from receiver, past from present, logic (the thought structure of discourse) from rhetoric (the social effectiveness of discourse), academic learning from wisdom – and 'Perhaps the most momentous of all its [literacy's] diaeretic effects...it separates being from time.'[25] All of this leads to a dominance of atemporal ontologies and epistemologies. A good deal of the material in the remaining chapters explores how these attributes of literacy have contributed to our madness.

Before turning to these more clinical explorations I want to briefly extend my earlier remarks on the relationship between p-orals and their language, and also comment on the nature of subjective experience in general.

primary

Primary orality's 'theory' of language

How might a person living in the p-oral state view language? I have already criticized aspects of Ong's tacit assumptions that amount to unwittingly believing that, basically, p-orals held views about language that were much like those in our received view. According to the schemes that I will develop, absurd as it might sound at first, in a sense, p-orals may not have had words, not even have had language. Of course, were it still possible for us literate folk to listen to p-orals speaking, then provided that we understood their language (which already loads the dice), we almost certainly would hear that they *do* have words – and syntax, reference, definitions; that they also have concepts that words refer to, such as right and wrong, true and false, self and other, good and evil, and so on. As previously noted, this is just what Everett found when he listened to and questioned the Pirahãs, both in the early stages of learning their language and later.

The alternative then, which I will eventually propose and consider is that p-orals did not have language, words, grammar, reference. How could one speak and not be aware of words; of grammatical structure and rules; of definitions and referents of terms? Quite so; that is my point. It is exactly our inability to even make sense of such a baffling, incoherent possibility that makes the p-oral state so unimaginable for us – just as Ong at times warned it would be. Under our present explicit and tacit world and language views, using language without being aware of atomic words, its fundamental particles or ingredients, and so on, is impossible, not even imaginable.[26] But let us remember that at first, and for some time thereafter, the very young child who has just entered the language dimension is exactly in this position: they are beginning to speak more or less coherently, can converse to some extent, yet are not explicitly aware of using a rule-governed, referential, meaning-carrying tool. It will be some time before they become indoctrinated

E-o rule
governed

into, infected by, the received view. Until then, the recently hatched child just talks and listens. They cannot yet say much if anything about what all of this involves, just as they would be unable to tell us much about their digestive processes. (I return to this point in Chapter 7 when I sketch a conception of a sane way of being in the world.)

This non-concept of language, what might be called the received *non*-view of language, lurks in radical contemporary philosophical thought. In various ways it is adumbrated in the thought of Heidegger, Wittgenstein, Derrida. Hints can be found even in the work of Quine and Michael Polanyi.

The paradoxes of subjective experience

Considering matters pertaining to p-orality and literacy has repeatedly brought up the question of inner experience – the differences that might exist between the experiences of p-orals and those of literate people. The issue seems legitimate. It is generally taken for granted that in both kinds of culture it is meaningful to raise questions about inner experience, that there is such a thing. It seems incontrovertible that all humans, whether p-oral or literate, 'have' something going on 'inside' (their heads?)[27] that one can properly call 'subjective experiences', that they 'have' some kind of 'thing-like things' – manifestations, appearances of something on an inner stage that each one of us can observe and then describe to others who can understand, who can make sense out of the self-observer's narrative, who have like experiences. Up to this point, much of what has been said tacitly embraced these kinds of presuppositions. We have considered 'what it is like' to be a neonate, or a p-oral.

However, things are far from that simple. The nature of inner experiences and objects, even their very existence, has been intensely debated for centuries, mostly in the context of realism/antirealism controversies:[28] is what we experience and perceive a direct view of outer reality, or are our observations limited to the observation of some inner events, entities (sense data, qualia, representations), stand-ins or representations for something caused by what 'really' is out there? In any case, what is the nature of this observer who observes and reports all of these experiences by means of language? In more recent times, there has been a drastic shift from such inner- or outer-object-centered debates to debates about language. How is language related to these inner or outer, and often non-linguistic (concepts, thoughts) realities? How can language refer, mean, 'hook on to the world'? Here we have the core paradoxes that plague efforts to understand experiencing. There is no end to theorizing about the nature of perceptions, affects, cognitive processes, conation, consciousness – and self, world and language.

Across virtually all disciplines, in one way or another, the current mainstream views about the nature of experiencing are grounded in one or another version of the so-called 'causal theory of perception'. This grounding is so commonplace, so taken for granted, that it is seldom even noticed, expressed or acknowledged. Under causal theories, perception is considered to be a subjective inner experience, inside the head, inside the brain which is the terminus of an event chain that begins with an energy emission from a source (typically some physical object) and ends with someone's perception of something (qualia, sensory data, phenomenology's phenomena, objects, pains, thoughts and so on). That 'someone' is perhaps the ultimate problem. Is it some kind of an ego (And what does that mean? What is that term's referent?), a temporary resting place along an infinite regress of receding homunculi, each one standing in need of explanation by yet another? So, the problematic issues of causal theories are: Who is it that is doing the perceiving? Just what is it that is being perceived? What does all of this amount to? Then, on top of all of these conundrums, there is the additional constellation of paradoxes raised by this elusive 'perceiver's' linguistic description of a non-textual experience, an event that raises the network of baffling issues about the nature of language considered in Chapter 2. So, under causal theories of perception we have an incoherent picture of experiencing that includes dogmatic and ultimately unintelligible conceptions of and beliefs about who it is who can report experiencing 'inner perceptions' of paradoxical, elusive, controversial phenomena and processes (pains, itches, feelings, wishes, reasoning, qualia, ideas, concepts), of an observer who 'directly perceives' objects and events in the 'outside world' and then reports this experiencing by means of referential language – a picture that, according to Wittgenstein, Heidegger and some others, is deeply flawed.

To say that this unquestioningly accepted model of perception and inner experience is a mess would be a major understatement. When looked at closely, causal theories fall apart. Here is Raymond Tallis's ironic description of the last stages of the envisioned perceptual process, a part of his extended critique of these theories:

> As a nerve impulse travels along an afferent fibre, it also propagates from one part of Roget's *Thesaurus* to another, a process that is accelerated when it manages to leap over a synaptic cleft and join its colleagues on the other side. As the impulse propagates centrally, it

leaves the world of 'energy transformation' and enters the world of 'signals' until, two or three feet and two or three synapses later, it has become 'information', or part of a pattern of impulses that count as information ... No explanation whatsoever is offered as to how this happens.[29]

Subjective experience is a horrendously vertiginous topic.[30] These days, experience qua experience is studied primarily in the burgeoning discipline of consciousness studies.[31] There, almost without exception the focus is on the brain and its activity – a comforting, simplifying, and very likely simplistic, reduction. Psychology and subjectivity enter by the back door, usually by conflating the languages of subjective experience and of neurobiochemical events.[32] (Raymond Tallis calls such devious sliding back and forth between mechanistic-reductive and psychological language 'thinking by transferred epithet'. He calls the field grounded in this practice 'neuromythology'.)[33] The basic problem may well be that as the philosopher Colin McGinn put it, 'The act of inner awareness does not have the phenomenology characteristic of a sense modality.'[34] Observing one's 'qualia' is not quite like observing trees. (I believe this is close to the point that Wittgenstein was making in his so-called private language argument.)[35] That, plus the problem of the ontology of language, is the problem of experiencing in a nutshell.

To my way of thinking, all of the paradoxes and apparently insuperable conceptual difficulties that one encounters when trying to gain a new, more insightful understanding of what David Chalmers calls 'the hard problem of consciousness' – basically, how energy impinging on humans' biological transducers and then traveling to the brain as neurochemical phenomena can possibly turn into subjectivity – originate in the ineffability of the neonatal state and in the move out of that state. This developmentally grounded view does not remove paradox, but to my mind it does situate it productively. Hatching is where experiencing as we know it – articulable experiencing – begins. That is where all of the future issues and paradoxes begin to take shape. Those are the fundamental paradoxical events that lead to each of us becoming a languaged person in a world that includes ourselves and that we can talk about. As we have seen, on this view, the familiar philosophical puzzles and conflicting views – say, the realism/antirealism problem and dispute – are debates about secondary, derivative phenomena, offshoots of the bifurcating move into the linguistic dimension that mysteriously turns neonatal (and perhaps p-oral) holism into (hatched, and perhaps literate) dualism. The kinds of problem we identify come into being only after the real puzzles have already been left behind. Accordingly, as I see it, if one is trying to understand experiencing, the focus ought to be on these originary developmental events – even if they are ineffable. I am suggesting that the starting point of our being in the world – hatching and literacy – ought also ought to be the point of departure for any attempt to understand that way of being.

We may be starting to get an inkling of just how far-reaching the consequences of developmental issues are. My contention is that the intertwined problematic phenomena of language acquisition and humanity's acquisition of literacy lurk behind, are at the core of, just about every scientific, philosophical and psychological issue. I believe that this is not all that difficult to see, provided that one looks deeply enough, and provided that one can suspend various dogmatic received views. At this point, perhaps my conjecture about the possible benefits that a drastic developmentally illuminated shift in our framework or worldview can yield may begin to seem more credible, although we still have some distance to go before we will be able to see the picture more clearly.

The next several chapters explore the ways in which the momentous ontogenetic and phylogenetic events that have been outlined in this and the previous chapter have generated, and continue to maintain and perpetuate, the pathology that I call 'humanity's madness'.

5
Ontogenesis and Pathology

Separating the individual and society

We may want to look at the pathology of individuals before considering the sociocultural pathology, but that plan immediately runs into difficulties. Thinking about these pathologies separately is unrealistic, and thus is bound to lead to distortions and misunderstandings. The great British pediatrician-turned-psychoanalyst Donald Winnicott wrote that he 'once risked the remark "There is no such thing as a baby" – meaning that if you set out to describe a baby, you will find you are describing a baby and someone else. A baby cannot exist alone, but is essentially part of a relationship.'[1] Much the same can be said of persons and society. They are two sides of a coin.

The point has been made in diverse contexts. The noted sociologist Norbert Elias said that 'self and society are historical, sociological, and psychological structures... indissolubly complementary and... understandable only in conjunction with each other'[2] and that sociologists

> should studiously avoid thinking either about single individuals, or about humanity and society, as static givens. The proper object of investigation for sociologists should always be interdependent groups of individuals and the long-term transformation of the figurations that they for with each other... [these] are in a constant state of flux... the foundation for a *scientific* sociology rests upon the correction of what he called the *homo clausus* or 'closed person' view of humans... and replacing it with an orientation towards *homines aperti* or pluralities of 'open people'.[3]

Elias emphasized that self and society

> are not two separate entities, but are intrinsically and irremediably interconnected. What is 'society' and what is the 'individual'? Both terms, Elias says, seem transparent and familiar, but upon examination turn out to be very complex... [Elias] sets himself against all views which claim that a society is an organic whole dominating the lives of individuals. He opposes with equal vehemence the methodological individualism which insists that individuals are in some way 'real' whereas social processes are not.[4]

Numerous thinkers have pointed out that this two-sides-of-a-coin relationship raises ontological and epistemological puzzles:

> There have been perennial debates revolving around the relation between the individual and society, or, what has also been labeled the macro-micro relation in social theorising[5]... the prevailing view among social scientists is that the psyche and the social reside in such disparate domains that their proper study demands markedly incompatible analytical and theoretical approaches[6]... theorists have long been frustrated by their inability to explain satisfactorily the relationship of mind to society and the ways that emotional and cognitive processes [in individuals] fit it[7]... collective behavior and social change have preoccupied sociologists and psychologists from the nineteenth century to the present[8]... [the usual simple (simplistic) referential use of the terms 'individual' and 'society' is] very crude and not especially adequate... *The relationship between individuals and society is something unique. It has no analogue in any other sphere of existence* [my emphasis].[9]

Individual pathology

Nevertheless, in spite of the questionable validity of making this bifurcation, attention has been paid to the mental illness of individuals at least since the time of classical Greece. Of course, the concept has undergone enormous changes, going from Greek theories about disturbances of the equilibrium of body fluencies (Hippocrates, 460–377 BC), to eighteenth-century ideas about moral insanity, to nineteenth-century concepts of 'romantic psychiatry', and to the present profusion and confusion reflected in a menu of theories and practices that populate the mental health industry. Current therapy approaches range from medication to eye movement desensitization and reprocessing, to revamped versions of psychoanalysis.[10] We might note, however, that to some extent the separation of individual from cultural pathologies is breaking down. Under various pressures the mental health professions – psychiatry and clinical psychology in particular – have had to begin paying attention to cultural questions, especially about values and norms. Important areas are diagnosis and assessment.[11] As minorities become more populous, criteria of mental health and pathology that over a long time had become established for, and by, the majority are being challenged. Difficult questions are being asked these days about the legitimacy of standard, well-established diagnostic tools and about the universality of standard nosological categories.[12] Long-established diagnostic categories are being removed, and new ones are constantly being added. Behaviors or beliefs previously judged by mental health professionals to be symptoms of 'mental disorders' are reclassified as normal, and vice versa. New categories grow like weeds. Currently there is a great deal of ferment about psychiatric nosologies, exacerbated by the recent publication of a new edition of psychiatry's bible.[13] Both pathology and its complement, mental health, have been difficult to pin down.[14] Statistical criteria for health and illness have been used because they are easy, convenient and apparently scientific, quantifiable, objective, sound, but they have also been criticized severely. (They certainly aren't presuppositionless.)

Many of the problems raised by cultural considerations reflect quarrels between absolutism and relativism: Is it legitimate for each society to set its own standards of mental health, or are there universally valid criteria? Are 'mental disorders' natural kinds, autonomous, or artifacts? Are they made or found?[15] If it is (statistically) 'normal' for the members of a society to be cannibalistic, or to see spirits, or to believe in what we Westerners see as 'magic', or to treat incest as natural and acceptable – or, for that matter, to torture prisoners, to sanction the killing hundreds of thousands of persons in seconds, to value pieces of paper and numbers in one's bank account over just about everything else,[16] to be indifferent to world hunger, to severely pollute the earth, or to entertain the option of mutual assured destruction, how are we to deal with such 'anomalies' – others' as well as our own? Are they psychiatric symptoms, or healthy behaviors and beliefs because they are the norm in a given society? The mental health professions have no satisfactory answer. How shall one decide? Are these issues more ethical, political, moral, philosophical, religious than clinical? Do they fall outside the domain of science-psychiatry-psychology-neurobiology-general medicine? And these are just the obvious questions.[17] We have a subject area filled with utter confusion – a mix of passionately held and argued but suspect, unresolved partisan beliefs, a spectrum of therapies ranging from 'scientific' (or 'evidence-based') to phenomenological approaches, and a raft of problems reflecting the questionable fact-value bifurcation.[18]

The conceptions of pathology and sanity that I will develop are significantly different. They are not based on mainstream criteria of mental health and illness, such as good social adjustment or the absence of officially recognized symptoms, although my notions will retain certain terms (for example, 'reality testing'). The atypical concept of humanity's madness that will eventually emerge arises out of considerations pertaining to infants' acquisition of language, humanity's acquisition of literacy and our current deplorable world conditions – origins and related criteria that are seldom considered in traditional mental health frameworks.

In the Preface to his *Philosophical Investigations*, Wittgenstein talks about the difficulties that he encountered when he attempted to present his thoughts in a linear, orderly manner, when he tried 'to bring all this together'. The best he could do was 'to travel over a wide field of thought criss-cross in every direction'.[19] I believe the reason why this 'wide field of thought' resisted his attempt at a smooth linear exposition was that its key phenomena and issues, mostly linguistic, were self-referential, reflexive and thus paradoxical. That is the case in the material of these chapters as well. In this chapter and the next, the essential phenomena under consideration are the pathologies associated with the infant's acquisition of language and humanity's acquisition of literacy – events resting on and raising self-referential paradoxes. The mutual interplay of individual and sociocultural pathologies is one of these reflexive features. Each of them illuminates, and is illuminated by, the other. (Individual development cannot be divorced from culture, nor cultural development from individuals; neither can the pathologies.) Therefore this exploration of individual psychopathology will not be able to avoid a certain amount of discontinuity and incoherence. Inevitably, matters concerning sociocultural pathology will need to be brought into the picture at certain points. (The emphasis will be reversed in Chapter 6.) Thus, there will be some unavoidable (at least by me) disjointed, discontinuous criss-crossing.[20] Here we artificially focus on the individual.

Evading genesis

As far as I know, before Freud, psychiatry had ignored early childhood development, indeed the entire course of individual development. There was no deeper model of ontogenesis. That omission, as well as certain post-Freudian reactions in the mental health fields that de-emphasized and devalued the role of ontogenesis in pathology, suggest that this pre-Freudian lacuna may not have been entirely accidental. At least to some degree it might well have been a manifestation of a widespread, time-less defensive human aversion and resistance to becoming aware of the experiences of early childhood. (In Chapter 3, I mentioned Freud's own aversion to exploring the oceanic feeling of early infancy.)

The more recent history of theory and practice in the mental health fields supports this conjecture as well. Now once more there is a near-total absence of thinking experientially about development and dynamics. It has been mostly replaced by mechanistic, tame neuro-biological models. Looking at infants' pathology has come to mean looking at neurobiological data. The deeper historical psychodynamic origins of mental disorders are elided in psychiatry's current nosological bible. That was not always the case. During several decades in the mid-twentieth century, psychoanalytic and even mainstream psychiatric thought and practice had paid considerable attention to early childhood development and its relationships to adult psychopathology. Even in that golden era of ontogenetic thought, though, there had been a grow-ing opposition to this kind of historicizing by conventional thinkers, such as cognitive-behavioral psychologists.[21] The developmentally ori-ented view of pathology dominated for only about 50 years. Gradually, perhaps beginning with some opposition to historical thinking within psychoanalysis itself, the psychodynamic perspectives that drew heavily on early ontogenesis were replaced by synchronic, atemporal, ahistorical frameworks patterned after physics – cognitive-behaviorist, humanis-tic, phenomenological, interpersonal, atheoretical/pragmatic – and by a growing interest in neurobiological models that retained only a shadow of historicity.

Today in psychoanalysis itself we find an emphasis on interpersonal relations, phenomenology, on the immediate present – a sure indi-cation of the underlying and mostly tacit presence of conventional metaphysics.[22] Today the mental health fields are dominated by numer-ous militantly atemporal, antihistorical approaches to therapy. The consensual views of mental illness are assertively ahistorical, reflect-ing the belief that paying attention to a person's history is not only unscientific but irrelevant: 'You can't change the past.' Thus, one way or another, the mental health fields have managed to avoid dealing with the threatening emotionally loaded issues of infancy. When these do come into view, they stir up vigorous, mostly unperceived and thus unidentified defenses and opposition that effectively restore the covering over of early childhood history. Typically, problems of infancy are turned over to one of the branches of (non-mental health) medicine or to biologically oriented psychiatry, typically for medication or other non-psychological approaches.

This ahistorical, even antihistorical, position fits in neatly with our culture's aversion to paying serious attention to the subjective realm in general. Deeper contact with one's self is evaded, and/or replaced with safe, maudlin navel-gazing or defensively driven hyperactivity. The severance from historical roots and issues serves to mechanize, physically reduce, depersonalize everything about ourselves, explaining our experiences by facile scientistic pseudoexplanations – typically, in respectable, safe, depersonalized neurobiological terms. Natural science's lifeless mechanisms become the model of the person. We have phenomena such as 'the decade (or year, or century) of the brain'. These models have no room for what philosophy and science long ago identified as 'secondary qualities' (a rose's smell, a sound's beauty) and exiled from the mathematized garden of Eden. What remains is a domain populated by inert objects and processes – state process formalisms. As I have argued elsewhere, the phenomena of the world of physics or natural science have no history, except in a very restricted, trivializing, objectifying, depersonalizing state-process sense. I have written a good deal about these issues and there is no need to revisit them here.[23] I did want at least to mention them as background for the considerations that follow.

Nevertheless, there have been some notable advances since Freud's day in the clinical understanding of the role that early childhood plays in a person's pathology. An interesting example is the fascinating work of Allessandra Piontelli, Professor of Child Neuropsychiatry and researcher in the Department of Maternal and Fetal Medicine at the University of Milan. She made extensive ultrasonic studies of fetus behavior. As her book editor observed, she

> does something no one has done before. She observes eleven fetuses... in the womb using ultrasound scans, and she then observes their development at home from birth up to the age of four years. She includes a description of the psychoanalytic psychotherapy of one of the research children and the psychoanalysis of five other very young children whose behavior in analysis suggested to Dr. Piontelli that they were deeply preoccupied with their experiences in the womb... Her central finding is that there is a remarkable continuity

of behavior before and after birth...Dr, Piontelli has discovered what many parents have always thought – that each fetus, like each newborn baby, is a highly individual creature. The newborn baby is not 'nature' waiting for 'nurture to interact with him. In Dr. Piontelli's view, nature and nurture have been interacting for so long in the womb that it is impossible to disentangle them; even the idea of nature and nurture as separate entities comes to seem much too crude to be useful.[24]

Her book about this work was published in 1992, and she published a similar follow-up study in 2002, this time exploring twins. Neither of these near-revolutionary works seems to have caused even a ripple in psychoanalytic thinking, let alone in other mental health fields, perhaps lending further support to my conjectures about the presence of defenses against deeper considerations of early development. If nothing else, her findings demonstrate an inextricable prenatal intermingling of nature and nurture that renders moot the age-old nature/nurture issues and controversies – surely an important insight. Still, the old, misconceived debates concerning this dichotomy go on undisturbed, untouched.

Piontelli later saw some of the children whom she had observed ultrasonically as fetuses in psychoanalytic therapy, and found linkages between some infants' observed prenatal experiences and behaviors and their post-natal psychological symptomatology, surely another important clinical datum. I have not seen any indication that her important, even revolutionary, work has had any impact on the mental health field. I have not been following the recent psychoanalytic literature closely lately, and so I sent out a handful of inquiries to psychoanalytically oriented colleagues asking them what if anything they knew about Piontelli. I only mentioned her last name, nothing else. Only one therapist recognized her name, and all he knew about her was that she had written a book about twins. This is a small, unscientific sample but it is suggestive. This apparent ignorance of Piontelli's important work can be read as yet another manifestation of the mental health field's strange (and, I suspect to some degree, unaware) opposition and resistance to delving into early individual development – and into history altogether.

Another example of largely ignored yet important work about very early phases of ontogenesis, much more radical than Piontelli's, is Stanislav Grof's work mentioned in Chapter 3. The cumulative clinical experience of this careful psychoanalyst/physician led him to startling views about ontogenesis. Time and time again during his clinical work, patients produced figures that looked like Jung's archetypes, and/or even memories of earlier lives.[25] The specifics of these improbable-sounding events are convincingly and carefully supported by copious data given in his challenging publications.[26] I mention Grof's (and Piontelli's) work only to show that the unconventional views of early development that I am about to advance may not be as extreme as they are likely to appear on first exposure.

The infant's crucial step

While there is disagreement about the nature and origins of the kinds of pathology defined in psychiatry's mainstream and defining categorization scheme (the nosology), there is a certain underlying commonality, much as there was a commonality – the received view – that underlay apparently diverse conceptions of language. Although there is considerable disagreement both about the nosology as a whole and about the nature of particular disorders, still there is a kind of broad, crude consensus. For instance, anxiety is widely (but not universally) accepted as a pathological condition, although the descriptive details and theoretical frameworks vary among therapists. So are psychoses and phobias. Psychoanalysts, psychiatrists, social workers, clinical psychologists, neurobiologists, pediatricians, school counselors all may vary drastically in their ideas about the origin and indicated treatment. Still, by and large they are likely to agree that Johnny is anxious, or has an attention deficit disorder. There is a kind of amorphous across-the-board agreement about the nature of pathology. The different views and approaches show something like what Wittgenstein called 'family resemblances'. Very few if any mental health service providers would characterize a particular patient as possessed by spirits, in need of exorcism – a conception that would not fit into the family.

I am trying neither to defend nor to criticize this family resemblance view of pathology and its genesis. The point I want to make is that, in any case, among all of these views and explanations of pathology, what happens within the short period of the child's entry into language, the relatively brief step of hatching, is neglected in the mental health fields' thinking about the origins of pathology. Even for those clinicians who do think about psychogenesis in historical-biographical terms, the pathology-generating eras of very early childhood are primarily those that came before or that follow this step. There is virtually no place for the step itself in psychotherapeutic thought. I suppose that one reason for this neglect is that the genesis of pathology usually requires some time, although obviously there are relatively rare exceptions, such as sudden severe injuries or other trauma. Since hatching and the initial step into language are relatively brief and apparently untraumatic phenomena, at first glance they do not seem to be pathogenic. What could go wrong? Why should therapists pay attention to this passing moment, this strange, short, low-key step into the language dimension? The unorthodox view that I will report is that from a certain perspective this step is precisely the locus of the child's entry into madness. It is the way in which a child enters into the language dimension in our literate culture that initiates the pathology.

How could such an ordinary step be severely pathological? Let us remember that this is an 'ordinary' madness, the pathology of civilized communities, a madness of normality. However, paradoxically, it is no ordinary madness in the sense that, say, schizophrenia is an ordinary (statistically normal, familiar and recognized) madness – it is unknown, unseen and its symptoms are, at best, misperceived (say, as virtues). It is extraordinary, extra-ordinary, one of a kind. It is the madness of our ordinary self-and-world view, of our ordinary, everyday, onto-epistemology – the madness of who we believe we are, what we think there is in the world and how we know it. Everybody is mad, so nobody can see that. (It is time to note explicitly that the mental health professions eschew the term 'madness'. It is regarded as an amateur's term, inaccurate, imprecise, vulgar, dated, judgmental, insufficiently medical/scientific/psychiatric. That is why I chose it.) The pathology is invisible because it is the norm – it is normal.

Almost invariably, in Western culture this step into the linguistic dimension is the birth of an explicitly initiated, and then abetted and supported process of pathological bifurcating that proliferates once it is in place. On hatching, the infant begins to learn distinctions such as me/not-me, self/other, inside/outside, name/thing – distinctions that in our madness we see not only as quite normal but utterly necessary, utterly sane, realistic. Language is at the center of this process. What is put in place of the previous ineffable, non-dual post-natal condition is an at bottom incoherent dualistic, paradoxical way of being a separate self in a world that includes that self as an object.[27] The failure to be able to make this body of distinctions is considered to be a symptom of major pathology, a psychosis. We remember that that is how Freud regarded the failure to establish firm me/not-me boundaries, except in the case of lovers and, possibly, of infants. ⟨Olafson p. 172⟩

Why madness?

What, then, is this madness about? To understand what is wrong one has to begin with the postulated earliest post-natal developmental state, a basic ingredient of the unorthodox picture of language acquisition sketched in Chapter 3: the neonate's ineffable state. Here, this infant's way of being state is assumed to be amorphous, unstructured, undifferentiated, non-dual (unitary), unboundaried.[28] The assumption here is that this unspecifiable, unimaginable condition persists until the infant takes the baffling step into the linguistic dimension, a step that is just as ineffable as the precursor state itself, but brings the child to a languaged state that we now can understand – or think we can.

One may well object to basing a conceptual framework on all of these presuppositions and paradoxes about infancy, but it should be remembered that the usual alternative – a respectably scientific developmental/learning framework of some kind – is also grounded in axiomatic assumptions, and that these bring with them formidable incoherences, paradoxes, infinite regresses. (Quite naturally, in our science-dominated age, they are bound to seem much more reasonable.) As even the logician Quine told us, within that usual framework we cannot know with certainty what our own language is and does, what that language supposedly describes, reports, defines, refers to, what meaning is, or reality, what other people mean, what our experience means. It is only that in our mad state we cannot see these paradoxical features of the equally hypothetical traditional, mainstream bifurcating framework and its concomitant received view of language. Usually the paradoxes and absurdities entailed by our normal commonsense views of being in the world are concealed, ignored, explained away by hand waving – mostly just go unnoticed. At least the present approach makes the paradoxical nature of its grounding, the neonatal state, explicit. Furthermore, I see this strange perspective not only as viable but also as more productive.

Perhaps we can already catch a glimpse of what could be wrong with the way in which a baby takes this hatching step in our culture – the development that is widely seen as desirable, a necessary advance in maturation, a normal step that in one way or another must be taken by every healthy human infant. What could go wrong when the baby says their first word, a gain widely welcomed and celebrated as a landmark achievement? What could it mean to say that the neonate is sane until it enters the linguistic dimension, to say that the hatched child isn't?

The position that I will be advancing is that what is wrong with this event is the ways in which it usually takes place in civilized cultures – that is, how the infant's entry into the language dimension is treated, how this hatching, the psychological birth as Margaret Mahler called it, is dealt with not only by the child's immediate environment but by the culture in general. I will eventually propose that the ways in which the step into the language dimension occurs in our culture is not natural but infected by literacy – not just by literacy per se but by the way it has evolved over millennia. I will then suggest that there are other, to us almost unimaginable, ways for the child to enter the language dimension, ways that could preserve and perpetuate the sanity of their original ineffable state. In other words, I will argue that there could be ways in which the initially sane infant steps into language and remains sane.

The other in the mirror

Let us look at the madness-inducing nature of hatching as we know it.[29] The mystic-philosopher Douglas Harding describes the situation well. He starts with a quasi-mystical sketch of the 'sane' prehatching state:

> As an infant you were like any animal: in that you were *for yourself* headless and faceless and eyeless, immense, at large, unseparate from your world – without being aware of your blessed condition. Unconsciously, you lived without obstruction from What you are Where you are, from your Source, and relied simply on the Given.[30]

The vague, poetic terminology seems appropriate for the description of an ineffable, amorphous, unstructured, unboundaried state.

Then that paradisiacal state was shattered:

> But humankind had designs on my native sanity. As time went by my parents persuaded me to stand aside from myself and take up their viewpoint, to leave [the unitary neonate] home and make the momentous journey from Here where I'm perceived to be No-thing to There where I appear to be a very substantial Something. They taught me that the character staring at me out of my mirror was not who I took him to be – namely, 'that baby over there', or 'my little friend who lives in the other bathroom behind the glass' – but was someone called Douglas, and indeed was me. With the help of friends and relations they taught me – and the lesson took many years and many tears to learn thoroughly – to 'see' myself no longer from where I am but from where they are, as if through their eyes and from their viewpoint.[31]

The psychoanalyst Jacques Lacan's description of the hypothetical era that he calls the child's 'mirror stage' echoes this view:

x Harding 2002, 1987

In recognizing itself in the mirror, the infant mistakes the image for itself, it misrecognizes itself. The clumsy infant identifies itself with an *imago* [an idealized mental image], setting into play the dynamic whereby the image will determine the infant's identity and future development.[32]

At first glance, this complex, obscure, largely ineffable step that is considered by our culture to be so routine and unremarkable does indeed seem to be innocent and desirable. Harding's step that creates his 'little friend behind the glass', Lacan's 'misrecognition' of the mirror stage, Taylor's step into the linguistic dimension, Mahler's hatching may seem neither pathological or all that important from a clinician's point of view, but in my view the consequences are momentous. As Lacan put it, the step does set into play a crucial 'dynamic whereby the image will determine the infant's identity and future development' – hardly an insignificant impact of the lesson that Douglas (or one of the two little Douglases) learned.

Lacan's setting into play of a crucial dynamic begins almost immediately on hatching (if not earlier), and it is noxious. Let us look more closely at what has happened to the baby Douglas. Almost overnight, the infant's unstructured world has started to become not only linguistic but fundamentally fractured and paradoxical, at least in the way in which hatching takes place in our culture: with this apparently normal, healthy, innocent creation of the illusion of the Other, the little Douglas behind the mirror, the foundation has been laid for all the dualistic, self-referential and other paradoxes that explicitly as well as tacitly haunt Western thought. Early in his important Heideggerian exploration, *What is a Human Being?*, the philosopher Frederick Olafson analyzes the situation and problems created by this dualist view of the person. On the one hand, we have the paradoxical 'I' that we experience as ourselves. This self is the reflexive, infinitely regressing observer of all, the observer who never can be observed. This philosophy's elusive entity has been given an endless series of names that actually tell us very little, if anything (usually it is called some kind of ego – transcendental, pure, empirical, psychological). Because they *are* names, they invite reification. These and similar terms are easily seen as referential, and thus easily can seem to give this evasive entity some substance, legitimacy, existence.[33] This elusive ego is the supposed entity that observes, names, recognizes, 'has' thoughts, ideas, pains, feelings, 'perceives' qualia or sense data or representations, identifies itself with its mirror other – the self that in an infinite, paradox-producing regression contemplates itself contemplating itself, comprising endless reflections in mirrors facing one another.

On the other hand, we also have the depersonalized 'other' self: the alter ego, the body-self that the 'I' observes, Douglas's little friend behind the glass. Then there are those others who apparently are just like him, raising the 'other minds' and a host of related problems. These others seem to be selves, capable of meaningful conversation, have 'I's, observing selves, but their inner life is not directly accessible to Douglas. He can't even be sure that they have inner lives, that they aren't fiendishly constructed machines, robots. Olafson's acute, extended analysis shows just how incoherent, logically inconsistent and paradoxical this entire basically bifurcating Cartesian foundation of self and world is.[34] One of its nefarious consequences is that it is the source, the archetype, of all of our familiar self-referential paradoxes – for example, those created by supposedly problematic sentences, such as 'this sentence is false'.[35] That is how humanity's madness becomes installed in individuals.

Trying to make sense of that 'I' raises an infinite regress (Heidegger's 'withdrawal of being', perhaps?) that leads one into a mind-boggling, vertiginous labyrinth. Awareness confronts awareness; language bumps into itself; inconsistencies abound. As noted, this notion of the self of which we (?) supposedly are intrinsically aware is the breeding ground of paradox and of error, as sages have been telling us for millennia. We routinely evade this unsettling paradoxical experience and the unanswerable questions that it raises by giving mechanistic, scientistic explanations for this supposed referent of the term 'I'. It takes a lot of hand-waving. These days the prime candidate for rationalizing this mess is the brain, split or other.[36] Both from an ontogenetic and a phylogenetic point of view, such scientistic, logic-grounded solutions only paper over this profound, necessarily elusive problem of the self, the fount of all kinds of distortions and conundrums. Deeply misleading and mischief-making pseudosolutions are offered, all sorts of illusions, pseudoanswers and pseudoquestions are generated and taken at face value. This has particularly noxious consequences in psychology. That discipline is supposed to take the psyche, this innately paradoxical 'I', as its basic object for scientific study. After all, that is what the '-ology' in psychology prescribes and describes. Can such a study be coherent? (The story is much the same for psychiatry.)[37] I have my doubts.

By the way, another pseudoproblem that this fragmenting bifurcation raises is the phenomenon generally called 'inner speech', the 'I' talking to – what or whom?[38] Ineffective scientific/scientistic attempts to understand and explain it continue to be made. Currently, these tend to draw on brain research, which may be interesting to neurologists or biologists but has little if anything to offer non-physicalistically oriented investigations. How can the unexplained observer (the scientist) relying on the unexplainable phenomenon of language explain what is going on in yet another observed self-observing observer? Surely it is reasonable to conclude that the entire picture of observing self in a world is fundamentally misconceived. Wittgenstein had reliable intuitions about this incoherence. He rejected and finessed this kind of explanatory enterprise in a number of contexts, perhaps most notably in his private language argument.[39] He recommended that philosophers should concern themselves with other matters. He abandoned ship, and turned to rather mundane and apparently less paradoxical everyday, ordinary phenomena and conceptualized them as language games, forms of life. His famous goal was to show flies the way out of their bottles, and not pursue ill-conceived, incoherent questions. I believe that similar holistic or at least anti-dualistic intuitions grounded Heidegger's struggles to reverse the forgetting of being, as well as Derrida's criticisms of the signifier-signified bifurcation. I will return to this issue.

The mad infant's mad helpers

Returning to Harding's little Douglas, let us note that Harding did not construct this illusion of the other in the mirror all by himself. As he said, 'humankind had designs on my native sanity. As time went by my parents persuaded me to stand aside from myself and take up their viewpoint…With the help of friends and relations they taught me.' Culture, adults, the Other, initiated and coerced the mad move, then abetted and supported it throughout life. Once the seed is planted, it blossoms, and the views that it generates seem entirely sound, realistic – certainly consensual. The conjuring act has become our reality. (This will be a core ingredient in my explorations of the idea of reality.) There is the 'I', and then there is everything else. Harding is very clear that there had been an external agency that had brought about his mad state. He is also clear about who that agency is: humankind, 'my parents'. This is one of the earliest major impacts that a mad culture has on a child, although one cannot discount the possibility that culture impacted even prenatal and prehatching experiences, particularly the experiences around the birth process, the domain that Grof calls 'perinatal'. At any rate, parenting of a certain kind is needed for the germ of this madness to be implanted, but currently it will be the rare parents who will not quite automatically fulfill their culture's expectations in that regard. Chapter 6 will explore more fully the contribution of culture to perpetuating humanity's madness once it has been implanted in the baby, and Chapter 8 will consider the ameliorative, beneficial role that an alternative approach to parenting and childhood could play.

I have been suggesting indirectly that the madness becomes implanted from the outside, but it is possible that it would arise in the hatched infant no matter what, in every culture. It certainly is possible that the mad split is somehow intrinsic, unavoidable, innate in humans. However, I will argue in Chapter 7 that there is some basis for believing that this is not so, that this mad split in the self is not inevitable, not innate, a possibility that I have already mentioned. We will see that there seems to be at least one sane, psychologically whole culture whose parenting approaches raise sane, whole children. Its existence argues against the hypothesis of innate madness.

Some consequences

Consider just how momentous the consequences are that flow from this simple, taken-for-granted step into the mirror world. As I said, it invisibly and treacherously establishes the ground for just about all of the conceptual messes with which we deal every day in one way or another (mostly by evasion). We have put in play the fundamental split of the self; the idea of conscious self-observed experience; the splitting of that experience into experience of self and experience of external world. But perhaps most consequential of all is that we have laid the paradoxically self-referential, dualistic foundation for the utter confusion about self and world. We now have an infinite regress in which the self necessarily remains perpetually elusive, the eye unable to observe itself.[40] The seeds of word-thing, referential, representational, rational-cognitive, separatist-received view of language have been firmly, irreversibly planted, and with them all of its incoherences. We have not only all of these difficulties about the self but, as a consequence of the bifurcations, we also have the perennial problem about reality, the nature of the outside world, the relationship between 'our inner experience' and the presumably autonomous external world of entities that gives rise to these, variants of all of the issues raised in the traditional realism/antirealism debates.[41]

From the ontogenetic perspective presented here, our entire conception of self and world begins to look suspect when we realize that it is grounded in second-order, post-hatching quasi-experiences, in illusions erected on the quicksand of the prehatched, inaccessible and irremediably paradoxical state. The illusions come with hatching as we know it and do it, with the ascent into the linguistic dimension.

The madness matures

After hatching and the planting of the initial seed have occurred, for the next few years of life the infant's understanding of the consequences and meanings that follow from their fundamental fragmentation remain at the level of something like Polanyi's tacit knowledge. For the first few years the child 'learns' implicitly, osmotically, mostly (but not entirely) without formal teaching. They are just a 'little scientist' learning mostly on their own.[42] (Parents do correct grammatical mistakes, for example.) Their 'knowledge' remains pretheoretical, unthematized, functional, not academic. The child is not yet able to formulate just what it is that they know. As maturation continues, more and more culture-specific matters enter the picture. I will not elaborate on these aspects of the development of madness here since they are the main subject of the next chapter.

I have come to see another commonly taken-for-granted aspect of our treatment of children as contributing to the child's growing madness. I will only mention it here since I return to it when I consider parenting in greater detail in Chapter 8. I am referring to our unexamined, dogmatic belief that infancy, and more generally all of childhood, is a special way of being that demands special treatment. To most of us, this way of looking at childhood seems obviously true and obviously incontestable, but it is a relatively recent cultural development, and it is not universally accepted now. This is not a simple issue and, as I said, it will be discussed more fully later.

At any rate, after a few years, the maturing child's madness now has a firm functioning foundation that continues to broaden and solidify the initially primitive madness. At some point, much of the child's 'tacit' understanding about self, world and language begins to become explicit. It is 'thematized' (becomes the subject of abstraction, theorizing). The previously implicit knowledge becomes more or less formal, conscious, available, able to be articulated. The child's starting school is one obvious landmark in this shift. Now the child can say that they know some rules of grammar. They can begin to articulate the values that they have internalized mostly unknowingly, can say 'this is right, that is wrong', 'this person is acceptable, that one isn't'. They now start to see language in the same way as does everyone else. They now know explicitly what words are, that individual words usually have referents and dictionary definitions, and so on. They begin to cognize everything.[43] The process of acquiring the received views of language, self and world continues; the ramifications proliferate, become sedimented and immovable. Most especially, the standard but incoherent bifurcated view of self as observer and observed becomes part of the child's way of life. Then, with further maturation, the child begins to assume an increasingly active role in perpetuating, supporting and disseminating the culture's madness. Gradually, each child turns into the culture's typical mad adult.

I shall summarize this elaborate account. At first, briefly, each infant's existence is an ineffable unitary and entirely natural, unreflective, unreflexive, integrated, undifferentiated, unitary, prehatching state of being that is exquisitely but unreflectively attuned to life. With hatching and the entry into the linguistic dimension, with the help of their environment, the infant enters an effable, illusion-generating reflective state of articulated duality, a basic self-referential condition capable of generating further self-referential paradoxes, endless speculations about the differences between (what one takes to be) perceptions of one's inside processes and states, about the existence or illusion of an autonomous external world, and about that mysterious element, the 'self' – an endlessly receding, infinitely regressing observing 'something', the eye that cannot catch or see itself. This secondary, derivative state that follows a sane beginning now becomes our culture's standard paradoxical, incoherent, yet unquestioned – and mad – view of reality. The paradoxical self-referential ego entity that plagues all concepts of self, world, inner events and states has mysteriously been created. The structural consequence of hatching is that a gulf, indeed many gulfs of many kinds, have come into existence. This primal but explicit, reflective split into me/not-me is the seed that (1) matures into an unending constellation of dichotomies and splits: inside/outside, true/false, real/imaginary, present/not-present, this/not-this, thing/word, this object/that object, this word/that word, mind/body, up/down, left/right, near/far, alive/inert, observer/observed, actual/imaginary and so on; (2) provides the basis for an unending set of specular paradoxical reflections (for example, about which of the inner/outer perceptions are 'real')[44]; and (3) is the fertile ground on which further aspects of cultural pathology can grow.

A reminder

We have been focusing on language and development in the past few chapters, and it might be useful to remind ourselves why we are doing so. We ought not to become distracted by these topics and lose track of our goals. Under the hypothesis of this book, in Western culture the step into language by each infant and the step by humanity as a whole into literacy initiates the growth of an endless network of mostly unrecognized, taken-for-granted and, in important ways, destructive, noxious consequences. Jointly, hatching and literacy plant and nourish a pivotal seed of madness, a deeply pathological potentiality, and under the culture's influence and with individuals' continuing contributions, that embryonic damaging nucleus proliferates into an infinitely complex self-world mad stance. It has consequences. One of these is that it has generated our current perilous condition.

To repeat, my thesis is that if we are to have a chance of finding a means of deflecting the looming threats, a profoundly different way of understanding our situation – that is, our understanding of self, language and world – needs to be found. However, that is impossible until we have become aware of our madness and begun to understand it – a necessary but most likely not sufficient condition for constructive change. Our aim is to achieve a radically different view of the globe's dangers, but first our madness has to become visible, real to us, more than just another piece of academic/theoretical, cognitive, abstract knowledge. That is the place for us to begin.

6
Phylogenesis and Madness

Group pathology

We have conceptualized individual pathology as a process that is initiated by the way in which infants' hatching or entering the linguistic dimension is usually dealt with in our culture, so cultural pathology has played a central role in creating individuals' madness from the start. It seems impossible to think of a mad culture without thinking of it as made up of mad individuals. So individual madness has likewise played a central role in cultural madness from its start. As shown in Chapter 5, the two pathologies are two sides of a coin. Nevertheless, we saw that looking at individual pathology separately was useful, as long as we did not take it literally, as truly autonomous, and remembered to introduce cultural considerations when necessary. This chapter reverses the process. We will focus on cultural madness, and the same caveats apply. The problems raised by that concept are the mirror image of those raised by the idea of individual 'mental disorders'.[1] We need to remember that there can be no autonomous, self-sufficient cultural pathology any more than there can be an autonomous individual pathology. We will criss-cross the field once again, adding considerations pertaining to individual pathology as needed.

Just as had been in the case of individual pathology, there does seem to be something to the idea of the pathology of an entire culture.[2] We have already caught a glimpse of one major apparently ubiquitous pseudoindependent cultural symptom when we considered pathology from the side of the individual: the way a mad culture engenders and sustains the radically distorting, estranging bifurcation put into play at the time of hatching, if not earlier.

At any rate, in spite of continuing criticism by many experts, the practice of personalizing or anthropomorphizing an entire culture, society or subculture – that is, turning it into a sort of superperson – has been in popular favor for a long time. Groups characterize themselves as well as their 'other', their shadow, in this fashion.[3] (The characterization of these 'others', the outsiders, are likely to be pejorative, racist, hostile.) These personalizations of groups do resonate with the public and even with some scholars. Nationalism, war, racism, discrimination, political parties and actions, team and school spirit, and the like greatly rely on such practices. In the present context an important consideration of the usefulness and credibility of such generalizing personalizations is the range of their application. That is, if we characterize a nation as, say, narcissistic, or authoritarian, or wasteful or dishonest, how many members of the group need to really be like that ('all Xs are Ys'; all Cretans are liars) before it becomes reasonable to personalize it? I believe that in the usual case, when one makes general statements of this kind about a group or nation, realistically that percentage is not expected to be very high (though the prejudiced person is likely to insist that it is 100%); the realist would be surprised if the generalization holds for 50% of the population. I believe, however, that in the present case the percentage is significantly higher. I submit that my characterization of humanity as mad holds for a significant portion. That is, the normal madness that I am about to consider is almost omnipresent in Western and Westernized cultures, which are the cultures I am focusing on here, the cultures that have brought us to the brink of extinction.

Background

The concept of national character, the ascription of individuals' characteristics to entire nations, became prominent during the second half of the nineteenth century, although it had already surfaced in the latter part of the previous century. The term 'national character'

> describes forms of collective self-perception, sensibility, and conduct which are shared by the individuals who inhabit a modern nation-state. It presupposes the existence of psychological and cultural homogeneity among citizens of each country, as well as the idea that each nation can be considered a collective individual, with characteristics analogous to the empirical individuals who are its inhabitants.[4]

Representative examples of such questionable attributions of personality characteristics to an entire culture are 'the crudely psychoanalytic character studies hastily produced in support of the allied effort in World War II'.[5] These unwarranted characterizations elevated simple folk notions to the level of scientific variables,[6] and they were based on a dated anthropology that made broad and questionable generalizations.

The views that come closest to my conception of humanity's madness are Freud's old notion of the pathology of civilized communities and Bartlett's recent formulation of the pathology of normality, theorizations that were mentioned in Chapter 1. In these versions as well as in mine, many behaviors, attitudes and beliefs that are generally considered to be ordinary, scarcely noticed, unremarkable, at most mildly odd – often even are regarded as admirable, beneficial – from this perspective come to be regarded as symptoms of pathology.[7] That is part of what makes the pathology 'normal'.

One of the significant differences between what Freud called 'the pathology of civilized communities' and the pathology that I call humanity's madness is that his, Bartlett's, and similar characterizations such as Fromm's, Kovel's or Lasch's are closely tied to conventional categories of mental disorder.[8] My notion of humanity's madness is conceived and grounded quite differently. A major difference is that although like Freud's or any psychodynamically informed therapist's, my conception of pathology is also tied to human development, here the nature of the developmental ties is quite different. In the present conception the two core events are those introduced in chapters 3 and 4: the phylogenetic event that dates back many millennia, and the ontogenetic event experienced anew by almost every infant. I know of no other conception of the pathology of normality that traces it to these intertwined roots. Another, related, difference is that language is the central element (both developmental events are heavily linguistic), and since the conception of language used here is original, so is the resulting pathology. These different understandings of the sources of the pathology of normality lead to a quite different conceptualization of the pathology itself, and ultimately also to new ways in which one might think about its therapy.

The idea that there is an aspect of humanity's pathology whose genesis goes back millennia (and perhaps also the companion idea that the genesis is tied to the infant's step into the linguistic dimension) may seem fanciful, but there is some indirect, surprising informal support for such an unconventional, long-term historical view of the roots of our current problems.[9] In a dialogue with the Indian sage Jiddu Krishnamurti, the physicist David Bohm makes an interesting and suggestive passing reference to 'something I once read about man going wrong about five or six thousand years ago, when we began to be able to plunder and take slaves.'[10] Another bit of support comes from the work of the sociologist and psychoanalyst Erich Fromm. In a discussion of recent slaughters and political failures, he notes that

> In these outbursts of destructiveness and paranoid suspicion, however, we are not behaving differently from what the civilized part of mankind has done in the last three thousand years of history.[11]

(He does not say what might have changed at that time, why he didn't see these noxious behaviors as innate, for example, but the implication that something changed long ago is there.)

So far I have mentioned several kinds of psychological-sociological-clinical conceptions of humanity's general ills. Just for the record, I want to mention another kind, one that draws on depersonalized science's neurobiological models. In general, in the present climate it is fashionable to explain just about all psychological matters with mechanisms that depersonalize, mechanize, physicalize, reduce. Behaviors, thoughts, beliefs and so on are side-effects of brain activity, what the brain secretes. Let us briefly consider two examples built on this premise. The first is Iain McGilchrist's major effort that proposes to explain our contemporary difficulties in terms of conflicts that have evolved between the two cerebral hemispheres.[12] The two antagonists are a person-like master (the right hemisphere), who has certain global, broad-focus competencies, and the challenger upstart (the left hemisphere), who was originally supposed to be the master's 'emissary', his helper, a second person-like entity who is more or less like a computer, precise, analytic, detail-oriented but disconnected from nature, depersonalized, concrete, tunnel-visioned. This emissary usurps the master's throne.

For me, this approach offers little that is new or useful. (McGilchrist claims that it has organized the phenomena, that the anatomy and the associated neuropathologies have suggested a corresponding psychological structures.) It anthropomorphizes or personalizes the two hemispheres (this is evident on almost every page), creating two homunculi who are in conflict. I see this as merely repositioning humanity's problems, restating or restructuring them in terms of two person-like entities that are embodied in the two hemispheres, as it were. As far as I can see, this tactic creates new serious problems and raises serious questions that remain unaddressed in McGilchrist's book. Who are these 'persons'? How did they get to be the way they are? Don't they have a genesis? What justifies personifying two halves of a bodily organ? We infer the presence of two opponents primarily (1) from the way in which brain activity is organized anatomically and neurobiologically and (2) from correlated behavioral observations, especially of patients with neurological deficits, but does that really make the personification of two anatomical chunks legitimate, defensible and, especially, generative? McGilchrist's characterization is useful in that it does call attention to our greatly excessive reliance on cognition, on our hyper-rationality, but I don't see that this neurobiological personification is any more advantageous in that regard than Louis Sass's older psychodynamically based work, a work on which McGilchrist draws heavily.[13] Let us also remember that although awareness, planning, conflict, competition and other human characteristics are ascribed to these two chunks of matter, nobody – and I do mean nobody – has the remotest idea of how an anatomical organ could experience anything. (We might well recall Raymond Tallis's ironic description, cited in Chapter 4, of the transformation of electrochemical activity into awareness as the signal nears the brain.)[14] And certainly there are others whose work has also identified excessive rationality as a major problem – for example, Heidegger's extended critique of the 'loss of Being', of subjectivism or metaphysics in general and rational-technological thinking in particular,[15] or Wittgenstein's ironic comment about philosophers' madness.[16] I expect McGilchrist's work to be highly appealing to reductionists, to be seen as greatly illuminating our circumstances. It certainly is a work of impressive erudition, but I do not see how it clarifies our problematic situation, casts any light on the nature of consciousness, or points to viable ameliorative approaches to the world's dangers. It provides another organizing armature or matrix for our experiences (but it also abets reductionism, as the author concedes) – and I believe that that is also all that McGilchrist claims for his model.

The second example of attempts to explain our predicaments via biology is the premise that in humans (and presumably also in other animals), aggression, destructiveness and similar behaviors are innate, probably genetically encoded. There is considerable evidence that this is simply false, that destructiveness is an aberration rather than the human norm, yet the belief is widespread and continues to persist, as do the accompanying contentious debates.[17] This is interesting from a therapist's point of view, and it calls for a comment. If an important but erroneous belief persists in the face of compelling contrary evidence, that strongly suggests that there are pathological defensive needs and processes at work. I take this unshakable belief about human propensity for aggression to be analogous to the currently ubiquitous, indeed near unanimous, belief that psychological distress, the mental disorders – anxiety, depression, attention deficit disorders, addictions of all kinds – are biologically grounded. I have commented a good deal on this matter elsewhere. Much of my book on substance abuse is devoted to showing the significant, defense-driven, pathological benefits that such depersonalizing, responsibility-disclaiming 'explanations' offer to many: patients, families, mental health professionals, drug and insurance companies, hospitals, school systems, legal systems, law enforcement, even legislators.[18] I will not revisit these mental health issues here.

One of the expectable objections to the thesis that I am developing, then, is that human destructiveness is innate, that the sorry circumstances in which we find ourselves are natural, inevitable products, and that my developmentally grounded arguments neglect this simple, biologistic scientistic 'fact', that they are naive, ill-informed. There are two answers. I have already given the first: the studies that call into question these mechanistic-biologistic psychology-disclaiming explanations, the kinds of explanations that finesse the role of persons. But, second, and perhaps more to the point, is this: even if humans did have a biological/psychological innate tendency to aggress, destroy, be 'evil', 'selfish', and so on, all by itself, this tendency would not – could not – account for our unhappy current condition. Any such tendencies would have to have become actualized – that is, the organism would have to acquire a great deal of power and control – in order to reach a point where humankind could manufacture global threats. Who would seriously argue that any non-human animals, even if they were innately destructive, aggressive (the supposed prototypes of the same attributes innate in humans), could be capable of actions that would threaten their own, let alone the globe's, survival? What other animal could have brought the world to its present perilous state? Why haven't animals ruined the environment, invented weapons of mass destruction?[19] What were they missing, and still are? The idea that other animals could be equally destructive is preposterous.

Similarly, could humanity even at the time of classical Greek thought – or for that matter, could scientists and technologists working even as late as, say, the nineteenth century – have brought about our present perilous state? Obviously not. Even the weaponry of the First World War, as pernicious as it was, could not threaten the globe and all life on earth. We also must remember that it is not just war that threatens our survival but also our destruction of the environment. And that is a recent and very human development. That until recently even humans, destructive as they may be, lacked the means to bring about threats to survival is beyond dispute. There must be some basis for these 'advances' that have enabled our current huge destructive capabilities, something that animals have lacked. There must be something that plays a critical role in our current dilemmas, and it needs to be identified. I propose that so far this noxious core agent has remained well concealed, and/or misidentified. If we can identify it, perhaps we then can also begin to think constructively about how to counter it and its consequences.

The literacy-induced madness

Here is a start. It seems beyond question that without the invention of literacy, humanity's history over the past several millennia would have remained essentially unchanged, more or less static. How could the p-oral way of life change the globe's condition drastically? There might be some relatively minor quasi-technological advances – the invention of fire, cooking, metallurgy, advances in bow technology or spear-making, navigation, farming tools – but without reading and writing, academia and formal schooling in general, professionalism, artisans, books, clocks, records, libraries, and especially without cumulative knowledge in science, mathematics and technology (in its ordinary, non-Heideggerian sense), our globe would not be, could not be, at risk, at least not from human actions. It is inconceivable that p-oral cultures could have developed the menacing states and potentials that we now are facing. When you think about it, it is obvious that, without literacy, such severely threatening circumstances are impossible. Even after humanity had entered literacy it took a long time – perhaps five or six millennia – and considerable cumulative advances in symbolization, methodology, social and economic thinking, and restructuring before science as we know it could arise. For example, to perform even the most rudimentary arithmetical calculations using Roman numerals is still almost impossible. And not much could be done in physics without at least calculus. After the rise of modern science, major advances in physics went hand in hand with major inventions in mathematics, enabled by new symbolizations and conceptions. To repeat Ong's point, it is virtually impossible for us to imagine what our world would have looked like had humanity remained p-oral; we have difficulty enough imagining what life actually was like even one or two centuries ago. It is exactly the madness-enabling potential of literacy in interaction with the madness that is installed with the infant's entry into the linguistic dimension that needs to be understood. I want to attempt to explore and explain this premise.

Let us recall what it was that Ong saw as the most far-reaching, sweeping consequence and feature of literacy:

> One of the most generalizable effects of writing is separation. Separation is also one of the most telling effects of writing... It divides and distances, and it divides and distances all sorts of things in all sorts of ways.[20]

He offers a striking conjecture and example:

> Eventually writing will create a state of mind in which knowledge itself can be thought of as an object, distinct from the knower... [Physical text is not knowledge] for knowledge, verbalized or other, can exist only in a knowing subject.[21]

Incidentally, one of the major instances of this distancing of knower from known is the distancing of language itself from user context – the position that in the context of the received view I called the separability assumption. Still, as important a manifestation of the pathogenic potential of literacy as this distancing may be, I do not see it as the most basic root of our dangers; we haven't yet reached the core characteristic that enables our self-destructive capability.

Separability brings about a loss of context; it *is* the discarding of context. It entails fragmenting, atomization, abstracting, a reduction and flattening of experience, generalizations. It leads to categorization, which according to John Ellis's acute analyses is a process that although central to cognition and competence is almost universally seriously misconceived. He explains that it is taken for granted that categorizing is the act of assembling like elements under a single label, treating them as an aggregate, a set, making distinct individuals into indistinguishable, anonymous members. He demonstrates by means of analyses of numerous important philosophical and linguistic topics (grammar, thinking, ethics and aesthetics, epistemology and logic) that this is not so. This standard, usually unspoken conception of categorization misses the boat, and that causes no end of mischief. Actually, at its core, categorization is a pragmatic move that consists of quite the opposite activity: it is a gathering of unlike items and treating them as alike for some particular purpose by placing them into a common set – a seldom recognized aspect.[22] In that way, items that previously had separate identities, were distinct individuals, differed among themselves, now become faceless, interchangeable, no longer distinguishable, just members of a category – but equivalent for some purpose. Therefore it is a potentially serious distortion of reality to take their equivalence too seriously, literally. It is a functional equivalence in some specific context, and usually it is a distorting misperception to carry that equivalence over into other contexts. As long as they are seen as members of a set, they become the anonymous Xs and Ys of a mathematical function, or the As and Bs of symbolic logic's axioms and processes. All of the items have certain features in common – reflexively and in a circular fashion, just those properties that identify them as and qualify them to become indistinguishable members of this or that particular set or category. Apples have certain properties; the category of apples is specified by the set of all individuals that have those properties. (This is the rigid logicizing that Wittgenstein sought to counter with his softening notion of family resemblances.) In some contexts, for some purposes, that loss of individuality may be just fine, while in others it may be quite damaging – indeed, madness-making. The trick is to know which case one is dealing with.

Incidentally, I believe that intuitions about the loss entailed in our science-dominated thinking have become more prominent in recent philosophical thought. Major examples are Wittgenstein's numerous comments about the need to place questions about language in context – use, forms of life, language games – rather than addressing them in terms of formal logic. As I mentioned, one way in which he criticized acontextual treatments of language and concepts was by calling attention to the extensive behind-the-scenes stage-setting that underlies so many issues. We excise, decouple, treat entities as autonomous and then obsess about them out of context, forgetting the precursor acts. That way madness lies. I believe that Heidegger, too, has an acute sense of loss of something brought about by scientism – what he enigmatically refers to as 'a forgetting of being'. He finds like-minded thinking in Suzuki's writings about Eastern thought, and is supposed to have said: 'If I understand this man correctly, this is what I have been trying to say in all my writings.'[23] Heidegger extensively criticizes technological thinking, enframing, apophantic assertions, calling attention to the shortcomings and dangers (see Chapter 2). He makes statements such as: 'Where anything that is has become an object of representing, it first incurs in a certain manner a loss of Being.'[24] Derrida's rejection of the referential concept of language – claiming that there are only signifiers and no signifieds – is another example of what I see as the

quest for unitary thinking and the abandonment of exclusively bifurcating our experiences. But, as I have indicated any number of times,
philosophers' thinking about these matters and their attempts to leave
dualistic thought behind have been, and continue to be, significantly
restricted by their neglect of and lack of knowledge about the developmental dimension. Thinking about the early infant's way of being
in the world, or what it might be like to live in a p-oral culture, may
make us dizzy, may lead to its own paradoxes and aporias, may leave
us at sea without answers, but at least it clearly identifies the context
of paradox, isn't alien, gives us a sense (or the illusion) that we know
what we are talking about (because both first language learning and literacy are familiar phenomena), and thus makes ineffability a bit more
accessible, digestible, less alien. This developmental grounding does not
provide answers; it teaches us not to expect any, and forces us to follow a *via negativa*. That can be productive. When one's familiar avenues
are barred, one is forced to transmute the usual rhetorical questions and
remonstrations – 'But what else can we do? What else is there?' – into
real questions and searches (of which more in Chapter 8). We have to
take seriously the possibility of alternatives, one that previously we dismissed out of hand – 'there are none'. It is also a way of helping us to see
the presence of paradoxes by showing that we do not understand events
that we thought we did – especially the child's acquisition of their first
language, and humanity's acquisition of literacy.[25]

Let us return to the matter of abstracting and categorizing. Through
these acts, much is irreversibly filtered out. It is as though one
has reduced a colored sculpture to a black-and-white photograph –
a leveling, impoverishing and unidirectional (irreversible) reductive
move. Individuality, distinguishing detail, qualitative richness, context
are irretrievably lost. In modern terms, information is lost.[26] Furthermore, in the course of categorizing, abstracting, formalizing, quantifying, theorizing, we are constantly naming and labeling, reifying,
inventing new 'things', concepts, attributes (of the set's members) as we
trade experience-near individualizing discriminations for abstractions.
We become disengaged by our leveling of the world, simplifying, decontextualizing, mathematizing, formalizing, casting phenomena into a
state process mold, depersonalizing and reifying – and distorting, often
severely. In this way we find (invent) new issues to philosophize about,
or to investigate scientifically (especially in the human sciences – see
for example the massive effort to illuminate the nature of consciousness in the so-called consciousness studies discipline,[27] a field that now
even has its own journal). So, in fact, we are actually losing a great

deal, removing much of our lived experience, even as we congratulate ourselves on our scientific acumen and the advances that we are accomplishing, on the cognitive and material advantages provided by categorizing, logicizing, mathematizing, abstracting, performing high-level sophisticated analysis. Worse yet – and here we begin to approach the roots of our madness – we are prone to taking the abstractions and their implications as 'real', even as we consciously and explicitly deny that we are reifying, deny that we are taking these abstractions seriously, as the way things really are. Our practices, theories, policies and our ways of talking about our selves and our world say otherwise. They show that we *are* taken in by such activities in many and fundamental ways. (Think of the enormously anthropomorphizing language invariably used when talking about computers: 'they' search, have viruses, compare, calculate, sort, find, wait, sleep and wake up. Consider also the absurd arguments over whether computers can 'think'.)[28] The reality-obscuring consequences of abstracting are surreptitious but far-reaching, and all too often significant and noxious. Ong perhaps unintentionally foreshadows this view when he says that

> Functionally literate persons ... are not simply thinking and speaking human beings but chirographically thinking and speaking human beings ... The fact that we do not commonly feel the influence of writing on our thoughts shows that we have interiorized the technology of writing so deeply that without tremendous effort we cannot separate it from ourselves or even recognize its presence and influence.[29]

The pathology that has become associated with being literate is compounded and expressed by the role that it plays in subverting the early development of individuals. Bifurcating, categorizing mad adults produces bifurcating, categorizing mad infants – adults raise little Douglases. We fail to recognize that everything we do, think, analyze, plan, even feel is dominated by the host of distancing, distorting, alienating assumptions that follow from living in, and having been hatched in, a textually dominated world.

This finally does bring us to what I see as the core of the madness. Without realizing it, silently and arrogantly, as we increasingly surround ourselves and work with fancy, sophisticated abstractions (especially in the natural sciences), we have traveled a long way down a slippery slope, increasingly getting to the position of routinely and widely (mis)taking abstractions and symbols for something that really exists, along the way becoming increasingly disconnected from our live, veridical experience of being a self that has a world. 'Reifying' is too mild a term for this mutation. What is happening is a mushrooming loss of contact with reality (certainly not an unproblematic concept),[30] a huge elaboration and magnification of the mistake that general semantics' Alfred Korzybski rather blandly characterized as 'mistaking the map for the territory'.[31] This is the catastrophe-enabling feature of literacy. Without the advent of literacy, this wholesale misleading and misguided formalized symbolization of being in the world, the bedrock that grounds the concomitant loss of reality, could not have evolved, or at least not nearly to the degree that it has: 'Without writing, the literate mind would not and could not think as it does, not only when engaged in writing but even when it is composing its thoughts in oral form.'[32] The penalties that this path ultimately exacts have remained essentially unperceived, unappreciated. Instead, all that has been recognized is literacy's supposed, apparently quite obvious, unquestioned benefits. Literacy, cognition, rationality, objectivity, theorizing are esteemed. We revel in abstract science and the concrete toys that is has produced (nuclear weapons and failing nuclear plants included). Sophisticated cognition is wonderful, but we also need to remember that 'The country in the world,' wrote the historian Hugh Thomas, 'with the best education for the longest, the nation with the most serious national preoccupation with learning, the people with the highest rate of literacy in the world in the eighteenth century were the authors of Auschwitz.'[33]

To recapitulate, my principal thesis is that p-oral humanity lacked the ability, the power, to bring about significant change in its environment. P-orals certainly could be what we might call locally destructive, cruel, dangerous, evil, but their capacity to do damage to themselves and their world was severely and fundamentally circumscribed by their lack of literacy and all that this lack entailed. They might have been cannibalistic, incestuous, aggressive, but they had to be attuned to nature in order to survive in a world that they could not control very much. It is worth repeating that they were simply unable to pose serious threats to the globe, or to humanity as a whole. None of all of the massive global threats that we have brought about and seem unable to deal with would have been possible before literacy. That conclusion seems absolutely incontrovertible and inescapable. Literacy changed all that went before drastically. Its ultimate effect, emerging out of millennia of development, has been to severely disturb humanity's sense of reality, to substitute abstractions at various levels for what is 'really' there, to erode what at one time was an acute awareness of and respect for our surroundings. Therefore, in a sense, our huge problems – even those of little Douglas – can be ascribed to humanity's becoming literate.

This phylogenetically grounded madness interacts in infinitely complex ways with the corresponding individual madness discussed in Chapter 5. Via parenting and related environmental impacts, it leads to the fundamental misperception of self and world that is implanted and grows within each individual as a consequence of hatching. After millennia of noxious evolution, the entry into the linguistic dimension goes wrong in literate cultures. In sum, this complex history and interaction of the two wellsprings leads generally to a stunted, distorted, unrealistic view of self, world and language. In turn, that gross, fundamental misperception of everything in terms of deliberate as well as unwitting, automatic abstracting gives rise to no end of symptoms, to manifestation of one kind or another that are widely misperceived, misunderstood, misascribed. It has played a major role in leading us to our current deplorable situation.

For example, there is some basis for the conjecture that under p-orality and in the earlier stages of humanity's evolution of literacy, individuals were forced to pay close attention to their immediate situations and to react in a timely fashion.[34] Under literacy, however, much of what we need to know or do will keep until later, to be looked at or done at our convenience – or so we think. We can afford to relax our attention – or so we think. We can write things down, look them up later, make notes to ourselves – and postpone paying bills, or paying attention to looming dangers. Referees and umpires can rely on looking at replays of critical moments in sports; events and decisions can be reviewed, and calls can be corrected later if need be. The upshot is that all too often the costs of not attending, of not seeing reality accurately, seem to be negligible, and so we have become blind to the present. Minimizing, procrastinating, ignoring long-term issues in favor of immediate and easy gratification, all become possible only with literacy. The p-oral's world must have been too close to the reality of nature to allow for these kinds of escapist lifestyle.

Under literacy and the powers that it has brought, problems and needed actions can be avoided for a time before their reality becomes inescapable. Almost invariably, misperceptions, denials, postponements, our failures to act responsibly, appropriately, in a timely fashion, entail heavy costs – eventually. And, since the bills come due only later – sometimes a good deal later (as we are seeing now) – we all too often have no pressing incentives to respond realistically, appropriately, in a timely fashion. We can indulge in fantasies, procrastinate and misread reality. The costly consequences may not become visible for some time. One needs to think only of Fukushima, the Gulf oil spill, the looming weapons arsenal, the poisoned oceans, global warming, fracking and just about all of the 'inconvenient truths'[35] that are so widely ignored or misaddressed (but the bills are beginning to come in). Hence also the otherwise inexplicable self-destructive behaviors already discussed in Chapter 1: corporations following policies and practices that superficially look like self-serving callous egocentrisms but actually will be destructive in the long run; nations refusing to renounce weapons, or implement ecology-saving measures. All that counts is the bottom line – that is our 'reality'. All of these kinds of failure can be seen as symptoms of a madness that blinds us to what is actually going on, substituting lifeless abstractions of one kind or another for 'reality'. In turn, these misperceptions abet all sorts of behaviors that may be immediately gratifying but are catastrophic in the long run.

In other words, in our literate culture, the costs of our widespread massive and continuing escapist maneuvers are delayed. By and large, so far there have been no immediate, inescapable, tangible penalties for our madness (or, at least, so we think), so our lack of realism, our indulging in defensive distorting maneuvers of all kinds, has gone unpunished.[36] In our civilization it has been possible to postpone taking the realities of nature carefully into account, to avoid being attuned, but the penalties that follow the violation of nature's constraints cannot be delayed indefinitely as we are just beginning to find out. On that view, it is our increasingly dangerous failure of what clinicians call reality testing – the ability to acutely and sufficiently accurately distinguish between fantasy and immutable reality – that is responsible for our present dilemmas.[37] We misperceive situations, substitute wishes for realities. This madness is profound. Later I will consider the impossible question of what can be done about all of this, but I do want to begin to point out that, from a therapist's perspective, it seems clear that our distortions of reality and their consequences cannot be fixed by more and better rational, logical-cognitive arguments, persuasions or explanations, any more than irrational phobias of an individual can be properly resolved in psychotherapy by cognitive arguments, behavioral conditioning. More than a century of experience in doing individual therapy tells us that something more than normal logic is called for in order to counter madness.

Literacy has had six or seven millennia in which to evolve to the point where its noxious potential has become a reality. At first its capacity to lead to severe, ubiquitous distortions of reality remained mostly unrealized (and certainly unrecognized). Literacy's dark side grew only as humanity's mastery over nature matured with the growth of abstracting science. Its consequences are all around us – but still not ascribed to literacy or abstracting. We persist in zealously maintaining the virtues of literacy and of what it has made possible (especially science and technology), oblivious to its undeniable nefarious consequences. The same is true of cognizing, abstracting. The issues are basically the same. At any rate, almost without exception the emotionally held and fanatically defended belief is that science and logical thinking are, if not entirely wonderful and beneficial, at least neutral, equally usable for good and evil ends. (I will later argue against this apparently unquestionable, unassailable belief.) Is this neutrality of science and technology not one of those things that is obvious to everybody? That we can build bombs as well as artificial hearts? This is a highly noxious, damaging instance of Heidegger's 'correct but not true' locution. It is another situation that leads to dichotomizing. We are convinced that one's approach is either rational, scientific, cognitive, factual and thus appropriate, or else mystical, magical, wishful and thus illegitimate, 'unrealistic'. When looked at from our mad perspective, the former approaches seem beyond criticism, and the latter ones unacceptable. The innate noxious features and consequences of scientism cannot be seen. To argue that what Heidegger subsumes under the label 'rational-technological thinking' has serious destructive consequences, that it is dangerous, is virtually incomprehensible to the true believers, to those dedicated to modernism's militant rationalism – and that means just about all of us.[38] (This situation is reminiscent of Condillac's inability to see Herder's objection to his conception of infant language acquisition, which was discussed in Chapter 2.) Heidegger tried to call attention to the unseen but deleterious consequences of enframing, the forgetting of being, technological thinking – to the kind of approach that, as he conceived it, converts everything, humans included, into depersonalized, stored fuel for future consumption, into a giant gas station. I am arguing for the idea that the received referential view of language, the incoherent, bifurcated view of self, the indefensible explanation of first language acquisition, the many paradoxes inherent in our dualistic conceptions of boundaries (me/not me, inner/outer) can all be understood as issuing from distortions of reality brought about by excessive, inappropriate, ill-conceived use of abstraction, formalization, modeling, cognition, distancing, separating – the everyday manifestations of what Louis Sass calls hyper-rationality and identifies with certain kinds of psychoses.[39]

Almost without exception this covert dangerous potential of rational-technological thought is totally ignored in proposals for dealing with our current threats. More use of natural science, technological advances and high-level planning are almost universally touted as the ways out of our dilemmas. The horrendous, demonstrated downside of scientism is not only ignored but, when pointed out, fanatically denied and contradicted by the true believers in Heidegger's rational-technological thinking.[40] Opponents are ridiculed as idealistic Luddites. If the unorthodox critiques have any merit, if science and technology are not neutral tools but always carry serious dangers, then looking at them as if they were the only, or at least by far the major, means of combating our dire circumstances may be neither beneficial nor innocent. Although the point seems almost impossible to make to the many fans of technological salvation, by looking in this nearsighted fashion at such salvation we may be committing ourselves to a class of 'solutions' that will only postpone destructive events. What we think of as solutions will carry the present dangers with them.

I realize that to those infected by humankind's madness, this point is bound to seem not only distasteful and apparently untenable, but downright perverse, a violation of commonsense. That rational-technological thinking may have an innate downside, that science may not be morally neutral, is just not acceptable. As I have said several times already, the cognitive-rational results of literacy readily masquerade as beneficent, wonderful, the ground for admirable progress. This view is fanatically defended; its appeal is huge, and so are its immediate defensive benefits. We see the defenses come to life if we even raise the possibility that science and technology may innately be greatly destructive.[41] A mild example of defensive reactions is Ong's changing views about literacy. After having specifically identified and critically discussed literacy's distancing, estranging impact, its negating of the warm p-orals' way of being in the world, he reverses and waxes almost lyrical in his admiration of literacy's benefits. He seems to have become blind to the downside of literacy that previously he had seen quite clearly:

> Without writing, the literate mind would not and could not think as it does, not only when engaged in writing but even when it is composing its thoughts in oral form...The technology of writing was not merely useful to Plato for broadcasting his critique of writing, but it also had been responsible for bringing the critique into existence...To say writing is artificial is not to condemn it but to praise it. Like other artificial creations and indeed more than any other,

> writing is utterly invaluable and indeed essential for the realization of fuller, interior, human potentials... By distancing thought, alienating it from its original habitat in sounded words, writing raises consciousness... We know that all philosophy depends on writing because all elaborate, linear, so-called 'logical' explanation depends on writing.[42]

Obvious recent examples are the scientific advances that have led to increasingly destructive instruments of war over the last century or so. Whether or not scientific advances necessarily have noxious consequences may be up for debate, but that they have had them, and that for many years the results have been horrendous, can scarcely be denied. Starting with the First World War development of 'Big Bertha' cannons and the primitive use of rudimentary war planes, proceeding to the dive bombers and rockets of the earlier stages of the Second World War, thence to Hiroshima and Nagasaki, and on to hydrogen bombs, advanced biological weapons, Chernobyl, and drone warfare gives us a snapshot of the typical explosive exponential growth of a destructiveness that would be possible only in a literate culture that has been evolving for a long time. (But then fans of scientism of course argue that we have hip replacements, artificial hearts, painless dentistry, fast cars and air travel, cell phones and the internet – and genetically modified foods, rampant obesity and poisoned oceans.) Isn't it strange and instructive that the presence of literacy is almost never seen as having had a part in bringing us to our present state? Again, science and abstraction, cognition, mathematizing continue to be seen as essentially value-free, neutral, equally useable for good and ill.

I am certainly not about to suggest that we should strive to return to a p-oral state. First of all, that would be quite impossible for any number of reasons. What I *will* be suggesting, though, is that we may be able to learn valuable lessons by looking at our madness and seeing its connections to the two momentous evolutionary changes – the infant's, and humanity's. (It is striking that both lead to enormous advances in abstracting ability.)

The core problem

It now begins to make sense why it is that we cannot seem to avert the disastrous looming threats. We now can catch a glimpse of how it is that we can know about Hiroshima, Nagasaki, Fukushima and Chernobyl, and still seriously even consider waging nuclear warfare; how we can continue to poison the globe and its population, to waste all sorts of limited resources, to be indifferent to humanity's widespread suffering. It becomes understandable why most major corporations pursue policies that are virtually guaranteed to lead to their own ultimate demise in the not too distant future, why so many people continue to eat food and lead lifestyles that are virtually guaranteed to make them obese and severely ill. Much of this situation is explained by a wholesale erosion of the sense of reality brought about by a complex constellation of factors grounded in the two momentous developmental events that have been the focus of this work. Fantasy has replaced reality. So, fantasy is what we deal with, what we perceive and value.

> Misdirected by two developmental events that have gone wrong, we now live under noxious received views of language, self, and world – views that are fragmenting, dehumanizing, depersonalizing, that distort and fracture the fundamental unity of being a languaged self in a world that includes that self.

Specific symptoms of this pathology are misperceptions in one or more of the three dominant aspects of that reality – self, world, language. All sorts of fragmenting, excising, decontextualizing are put in play. For example, we begin to take referential talk about our 'inner events' seriously, and start to argue about their nature – the kind of move that Wittgenstein tried his best to discourage in philosophy. A previously integrated, precognitive, prethematizing, smooth, tacit attunement of self, nature and language – the way of p-orality, I believe – becomes thematized. Our way of being in the world becomes structured, cast in terms of a paradoxical self interacting with paradoxical formal-logical-mathematical-physicalist autonomous, decoupled, distanced, abstracted and theorized-about (pseudo)objects. What we think of as our selves isn't real, and neither are what we think of as that self's objects (the term taken in the widest sense, the psychoanalytic one included). It is difficult to recognize just how ubiquitous the symptomatic manifestations of humanity's madness are. A formalized, abstract, dehumanizing way of life, Heidegger's rational-technological, enframing thinking, comes to be seen as normal, sane, desirable, constructive, valuable – realistic. All alternatives to enframing are considered to be fuzzy-minded, mystagogical, soft-headed.

A key impediment to any remedial efforts is that as seen from our distorted, received-view perspective, the loss of reality testing that has occurred is invisible. In Korzybskian terms, what has happened is that all maps have come to be taken as territories. The actual territories have disappeared from view, and their loss is invisible. As a result of unending interactions between the two momentous developmental moves that have gone massively awry, we have come to live in a world of maps, abstractions that we take for reality. We have become mad, and, paradoxically, that madness is just about impossible to see when one is mad. It is 'the pathology of civilized [literate] communities', 'the pathology of normality'.

Reality

The time has come to take a closer look at the key term 'reality", which I have been tossing about so casually from the beginning. For philosophers, reality/realism has come to mean some version of a particular complex view of the world. Perhaps its key feature is the 'external world's autonomy – it is what it is, regardless of what we do, think, wish, believe, say. That is only the tip of the iceberg. Lee Braver, in his magisterial exploration of the realism-antirealism controversies that have been going on at least since the time of classical Greek thought, extracts six defining features of realism that he calls its matrix.[43] Antirealism is defined negatively, as any view of the world that denies realism. It, too, has a six-element matrix. Then there are all sorts of mixed positions that use parts of both matrices. Obviously the concept of reality is highly problematic, at least to many philosophers and deeper thinkers.

The key factor in my argument is that, invariably, the versions of realism and antirealism that Braver examines – and there are many – still retain the key features of the received view of language, and all that goes with it. The realism matrices and the debates around them rely on the standard dichotomies: word/thing, subject/object, internal/external, right/wrong, true/false, thoughts and things; concepts such as existence, knowledge, intellect; and language as referential, descriptive – the separatist's conception of language as the autonomous tool. The antirealism matrices refer to mind, consciousness, feelings, truth, thought, object and subject, the 'I' and its predicates, appearances and the active knower who 'has' them. Both realists and antirealists thematize the problem of reality, explicitly make it the object of formalized, logicized theory, analysis, criticism. Being good philosophers, that is what they do. It is beyond my competence to address the question of whether radical thinkers, Heidegger in particular but also others such as Wittgenstein, also operate within this ontoepistemological framework, within 'metaphysics'. It seems that the issue is controversial. Philosophers who are interested in drastically changing their framework, in escaping this old dualism, routinely seem to accuse each other of having failed to do so. My opinion is that they try to escape the framework but are stuck. As I have said several times, I believe that the core problem is their inability or disinclination to address developmental issues.[44]

The view (or theory) of reality that I am trying to present is much like Wittgenstein's and Heidegger's theory of language: there isn't any, I don't have any. The reality that madness distorts is a prethematized, preconceptualized, tacit, unreflected and unreflexive, implicit something. It can be defined only negatively, in much the same way as the neonate's ineffable state, and the p-orals' unknowable state. So, what I am offering is a non-theory of reality, or, if you like, a negative definition: *neti, neti*. (Informally, regardless of what one may think 'it' is, reality is that something that if and when it is misperceived or ignored is sure to come back to haunt you.) I will expand on the question of reality further in Chapter 7.

Examples of symptoms

One basic premise of this book that has been expressed in various ways and contexts, a constant theme, is that symptoms of humanity's madness are everywhere, but are either overlooked, because they appear to be just normal and ubiquitous, ordinary actions or beliefs, or noticed, but not regarded as particularly pathological, seen perhaps as just mildly undesirable or inconsiderate (sitting in a parking lot with the car's engine and the air-conditioning running), or even regarded as admirable (fervent nationalism; being a good consumer; supporting one's country's military efforts). The geneses of many actions and beliefs are misperceived. They are not recognized as particular manifestations of a severe underlying fundamental distortion of reality, of what is really a very worrisome, dangerous foundation.

The real-world consequences of the symptoms vary greatly. Some symptoms carry severe penalties, while the impact of others might be trivial. Nevertheless, symptoms are symptoms, and from a diagnostic point of view they are equally worrisome because of what they imply – in the present instance, the presence of a destructive, general 'ordinary' madness. What follows is a sampling of what I see as its symptoms. I begin with some of those that I see as having the most severe material, physical, tangible actual consequences in the real world, continue with some whose real-world consequences are significant but not quite as catastrophic, and conclude with examples of symptoms that are primarily observable in the psychological realm, that have to do with one's so-called inner world (but whose ultimate deleterious impacts are nevertheless quite tangible).

The most obviously damaging severe symptoms are those discussed in Chapter 1, the ones pertaining to nuclear war and environmental catastrophe. I offer Al Gore's bland explanations of humankind's failures to adequately address global warming as an example of misperceptions of the true ground of the behaviors in question: the distancing from reality. Here are his explanations of why we haven't done better in countering these threats (but, to his credit, he is very clear that he does not yet have 'all the answers'):

> I spend a lot of time asking myself that question, and one dimension of my failure is that I don't yet know all the answers to that question... I don't want to give you the impression that we haven't had a lot of movement. It's just that nothing has yet matched the scale of the response that is truly needed. Why has it taken so long for this message to sink in? Number one, the unprecedented nature of this crisis does make it difficult to communicate. We naturally tend to conflate the unprecedented with the improbable, and nothing in our prior history or cultures prepares us for the reality of this radically new relationship between human civilization and the Earth... Number two, the garden variety denial that psychologists tell us we all fall prey to. [*This* psychologist wouldn't put it in just that way...] It's hard to sustain the focus of a global community on a challenge that is difficult and sometimes painful to think about. Number three, it's difficult to imagine engineering the scale of the changes that are now necessary on a global basis... Fourth, there has been a well funded, sophisticated effort to intentionally slow down the progress of this message... And the final cause would be, those of us trying to communicate haven't yet found sufficiently effective ways to get the message across. But we will and I come back to the encouraging signs we are making progress.[45]

Our gross distortions of reality aren't recognized. Each of the factors for our lack of success in countering these inconvenient truths mentioned is described in a lukewarm fashion ('difficulty of communication'; 'garden variety denial'; 'sophisticated effort to slow down progress'; ineffective communications). Gore's message is pervaded by the unjustified tone of optimism that is likely to follow when the current scene is minimized because it is being viewed through our reality-distorting spectacles (and when one is hoping to keep people comfortable and happy, and to sell books). There is no clear expression that we are facing an extreme, desperate situation that ought to scare us to death. Instead we have his Pollyanna-ish 'we are making progress' reassurance. Indeed.

Similar remarks apply to our ways of dealing with the dangers of nuclear war. We don't really let ourselves see the realities, or the part that we ourselves play in creating them. It is always the Other. The danger becomes depersonalized, and to that extent abstracted away. People's actions become 'The nuclear threat' – a vague, depersonalized, out-there menace that we cannot come to grips with. It is a threat from Mars. We have nothing to do with it. If we were to see the threat for what it is, *our* threat, we would begin by not tolerating even considering waging such a war. We would not tolerate 'keeping our nuclear options open' while forbidding others to obtain these weapons, threatening to enforce this prohibition by drastic actions. Instead of starting with ourselves, our own role in this mess, our preventive moves focus on all sorts of conventional, tried and untrue countermeasures, such as treaties, incentives, military action and so on. We look elsewhere, outside. Almost never do we raise the basic question for all concerned, for ourselves as well as for our identified enemies: How is it possible that a sane person, or a sane country, can seriously contemplate waging nuclear warfare, a move that is likely to end most, if not all, human life on the globe? One of the questions that we ought to raise instead of negotiating treaties is how any politician, military leader or industrialist can seriously rely on mutually assured destruction (appropriately referred to as MAD) as a preventative. Is that crazy response really all we can think of? What does that say about humanity's sanity or inventiveness? Or about its perception of reality? Were we to start with the obvious and only sane position that nuclear war is simply not an option for anyone, we would be forced to look more imaginatively and urgently for another more promising, reality-oriented and radically different approach. We would not be grossly misled by putting our hopes in adequate armaments and threats. We would not be satisfied with claims that we are trying everything possible. Our distortion of reality clouds that search for a solution. Ironically, instead it is giving up the nuclear option that comes to be seen as unrealistic and weak, dangerous. That is pathetic. Our approach must begin with the realities, with that which is widely regarded as idealistic, unrealistic: the unshakable position that it is absolutely mad, unrealistic, devastating to even contemplate that kind of combat – but then, we would have to recognize our own madness. There is more that follows from this approach to reality, and it will be considered in chapters 7 and 8.

An important but less directly globe-threatening symptom is our attitude toward the area of money, economics, jobs. Money 'has' value. If it is available, one can get things; if not, one can't. We can save it or spend it. We dedicate all of our efforts toward acquiring and saving it. It is more real than real. Creating jobs seems to have absolute priority – another symptom of madness, mad values. Money matters and creating jobs are much more important than survival matters – what could be more insane? In reality, first of all, money is a squiggle of sorts – pieces of paper or metal, marks on a ledger that have become symbolic, magical. Its strange true nature and value are widely misperceived. If one begins to look more deeply into just how it comes into being and then is manipulated, it becomes apparent that, ultimately, money is chimeral, a magic-ridden, weird figment of our collective imagination.[46] Trying to make sense of its genesis and history is a vertiginous experience.[47] It has no material reality or value. It is symbolic – but of what? Of gold deposits that back it – something else that is magical and whose realities are equally badly distorted? Why do we value items such as gold? So, we have baffling, incoherent situations. For instance, one day everything may be going along as usual, much is being accomplished. Then there is some sort of a financial crisis, a purely symbolic, abstract event where little if anything real has changed in our world – mostly changes in squiggles somewhere, somehow, and certain persons' reactions to these. Now suddenly all kinds of real-world material projects that had been viable and ongoing are no longer possible. Construction has to stop: 'there is no more money' for it. Yet nothing substantial has changed in the world's realities, other than a lot of changes in what mad people regard as their real world – changes in certain squiggles, beliefs, and policies.[48] Yet, just about everyone accepts this kind of situation as reasonable, utterly realistic. Something really has gone wrong, and needs to be fixed, we all think. Instead of questioning the reality of what has happened, we worry about how to repay debts, lower (or raise) interest rates, secure more loans, create more jobs, get more education when people who are already well educated cannot find jobs. In such scenarios, hardly anyone questions that something drastic has changed in the actual realities of self and world. Abstractions dominate our lives.

Another example is the routine anthropomorphizing of computers, a phenomenon that I have already mentioned. Some experts seriously maintain that computers can think, will turn out to be human because future computers will be able to pass the so-called Turing test: if you 'say' something to some as yet unidentified entity hidden in the next room, and if you are unable to decide whether that entity's response is coming from a person or a computer, then that entity is said to be thinking. That might be a legitimate definition of thinking in some technological, scientific or mathematical-logical disciplines for some limited purposes, but why on earth would anyone take this 'test' seriously as a criterion for establishing whether that entity next door is human? (I'd just as soon go next door and have a look.) On that basis one can argue that Deep Blue, the chess-playing machine, is thinking. Kasparov couldn't be sure that it wasn't a person who defeated him. Is this not madness? One can maintain that a computer thinks only by totally ignoring the huge amount of Wittgensteinian prior stage-setting that has gone into the technology that makes the machine possible. That stage-setting might well include the entire history of Western scientific, mathematical, logical and technological thinking and doing, as well as the many decades of more recent theoretical and empirical developments and advances in computer science specifically. Other noxious consequences that stem from this mad misperception and contention of what computers are, and can do, are the deleterious effects that result from their use by children, especially very young children – a large, obscure and complex topic.[49] The effects can be very subtle and covert, but nevertheless serious. As a therapist I have seen strange, catastrophic yet virtually invisible conflating of realities and media events in patients who on the surface seemed to be well functioning, their madness – the underlying tenuous sense of reality – well covered over by apparently quite normal behavior.

Before leaving the subject of computers I want to at least mention another troublesome consequence of our unrealistic views about them. Increasingly they are being used to make decisions that can have severe life and death consequences. For example, we have assigned computers the responsibility of 'telling us' whether, or when, to launch missiles. Making key financial decisions is a less catastrophic but similar example. The justification is that such decisions are supposedly scientifically based, the outcomes of 'inferences the computer draws objectively on the basis of available data' (another mad anthropomorphization). The programmers and politicians who remain in the middle of these decisions have become invisible, as has the military chain of command that decided to turn over its decision-making responsibilities to a machine. This is separability, fragmentation, isolation, depersonalization, gross distortion of reality with a vengeance. What is occluded here is our becoming aware that behind or underneath such formalistic, computation- and logic-based, apparently 'objective' and near-infallible computer 'decisions' there are fallible, invariably prejudiced, hyper-rational, dogmatic mad humans who now are able to disclaim responsibility. They only did the math; the computer did the rest. Hal from *2001: A Space Odyssey* has arrived (but his disabler has not). One hears all sorts of rumors of near disasters, nuclear missiles that were almost launched as counterstrikes and could have started the Third World War, all on the basis of what turned out to be computer glitches. This is not an isolated situation. By now there are probably few major important military, corporate or government decisions that are relatively free of this kind of mechanical-computational depersonalized interference. Can one really defend these kinds of action as sane, optimal? Is this the best we can do in response to dangerous realities?

Another strange phenomenon that is so common as to be taken as normal, reasonable, is the disproportionate reaction to individuals' tragedies. Although such responses are widely seen as compassionate, appropriate, they express a significant pathological distortion of reality. (That view may seem perverse – see Chapter 8.) Almost daily, somewhere a child, pet, wild animal or adult suffers some grievous injury or injustice, becomes seriously ill, gets killed. Somehow, this one undeniably lamentable incident captures the nation's or even the world's interest and sympathies, and assumes great importance – briefly, for its 15 minutes of fame. Articles are written, principals are interviewed, action is solicited, the internet goes viral, help is offered, money is raised. Now all of that may be well and good. Nobody would deny that these kinds of lamentable event are worthy of concern and support. What I see as pathological is that this practice is patently disproportionate, grossly unbalanced, does not take reality into account. Every day there also are hundreds, if not thousands, of other individual tragedies all over the globe. Not only a great many people but also untold numbers of non-human animals – for instance, those we are raising for slaughter, or are injured or killed by our destruction of the environment – suffer equally horrendous fates and are mostly ignored. Isn't it greatly unrealistic, falsely sentimental, to single out one eye-catching instance of a tragedy, pour considerable resources into ameliorative attempts, agonize over it, while at the same time turning a blind eye to the innumerable other equally lamentable tragedies that are occurring all over the world? Yet, as I say, this gross imbalance is commonplace, accepted as entirely natural, even laudable and humanistic. I haven't seen it challenged. (This challenge may very well provoke outrage.) What kind of defensible rationale could support this gross skewing of attention and support, this outpouring of emotion, while at the same time we are being callously indifferent to the massive number of other tragic events? Are these skewed perceptions and responses really justified by lame rationalizations ('I can only do so much . . . ')? I believe that the distortions allow us to feel falsely virtuous about how much good we are doing, while at the same time enabling us to avoid feeling guilty, helpless and deeply distressed over humanity's plight (as we ought to be), to avoid having to face up to our world's conditions and our responsibilities.

The numerous critical comments about our default view of language that were made in the earlier chapters identified separatist aspects of our beliefs about what language is and does, but they did not emphasize the reality-distorting effects of separatism, and in that sense the madness of the default view. I want to give an example of a madness that can only arise in literate societies, since it pertains to written text. In a way, it is a core ingredient of that madness, its very prototype. We look at a written 'word' and see/think a word, unaware of the obvious fact that what we are looking at is 'really' only a squiggle, something that is totally meaningless in and by itself. The squiggle has usurped reality. (The same goes for the acoustic signal we call speech.) We forget the great amount of Wittgensteinian stage-setting that has gone into the 'writing' and 'reading' of that squiggle, and once again take the map for the territory. Our madness makes what realistically are innately meaningless physical marks into an (apparently) meaningful word. We fail to remember, assuming that we ever knew, that our automatic 'understanding' of such innately meaningless squiggles or their acoustic equivalent is rooted in a very long history. Someone had to make that squiggle. In turn, that act must have been preceded by a lifetime of experiences and learning. These made it seem to the writer and reader that the squiggle was meaningful all by itself, that 'it said something' – and, for that matter, that this 'word', that squiggle all by itself, on its own, 'stood for' something, had a referent, a signified.

The actual background of both writer and reader that makes the apparently simple act of reading a word possible is both staggering and invisible. This is the kind of mad misperceiving that leads us to take as real, and agonize about, 'self-referential sentences' such as 'this sentence is false', or mathematical proofs such as those leading to Gödel's paradoxes. We isolate them, then take them as real and autonomous entitites, or at least as real enough to analyze and debate 'them' and their logic endlessly. Worse, in such contexts we have come to regard any reference to the human element as unacceptable psychologizing. We take it for granted that these squiggles are bits of analyzable data and, although isolated, still meaningful in themselves. And then we are amazed to discover that 'sentences can refer to themselves', have meaning, and we argue endlessly about how that can be. I have discussed these matters elsewhere.[50] Some have argued, defensively, that my contentions about distortions of reality are silly, that, for example, no one in their right mind would take such squiggles for anything but squiggles. That may be so in a sense. I suppose that were one to ask persons formally, explicitly, officially, whether they think some ink mark 'is' something other than that mark – say, a word, a concept – chances are they might say no because that is the expected answer. However, that is a superficial view of the situation, again an example of Heidegger's 'correct but not true'. I would bet that at the levels at which these issues matter, in spite of such protestations, squiggles do have meaning for individuals, at some levels are seen as existing and meaningful on their own. We have here yet another example of a Korzybskean mistaking of the map for the territory.

A closely related mad issue concerning language is the general problem of the referent – the problem that both Derrida and Wittgenstein 'solved', each in his own fashion, by dismissing the problem of the signified. I will not discuss this difficult issue here, but only note that, once again, it can only have become the paradoxical problem in philosophy and linguistics (and, peripherally, almost everywhere else – for example, in quantum physics) as a result of the separability assumption. In their usual formulations, paradoxical problems about signifiers arise in a depersonalized context. Persons have been removed. The excised squiggle and its obscure, problematic referential world have become autonomous. The mathematical equation refers, all on its own. All of these are cases of mad ways of being in the world, of being captured, misled, and incapacitated by abstractions.

The same considerations apply to speech as well. In too many situations what is said takes on a strange material reality. Fights, murders, lawsuits, even wars are precipitated by what someone has, or has not, said.

Finally, let me mention symptoms of our madness that concern ourselves as experiencing entities, selves. Here are two examples. The mid-seventeenth-century philosopher, theologian and mathematician Blaise Pascal wrote in his *Pensées*: 'I have often said that the sole cause of man's unhappiness is that he does not know how to sit quietly in his room.' With this intuition he anticipated one of the common and apparently unremarkable phenomena that I see as further symptoms of our madness: the widespread and taken-for-granted near absence of what the important early psychoanalyst Donald Winnicott called 'the capacity to be alone'.[51] (Winnicott was the first pediatrician to become an analyst. Many therapists, myself included, have found his views of infancy and early development to be invaluable clinical guides.) According to his developmental views, this capacity not only to tolerate but to welcome and be comfortable with being alone is acquired only by an infant who has had early experiences of ongoing benign parenting, the experience of safely 'being alone in the presence of someone', as Winnicott put it. Infantile fears of catastrophic abandonment, common if not inevitable in our culture at least, must be countered experientially. No amount of later cognitively based reassurance and arguments will do. There is no need to elaborate on Winnicott's developmental/clinical thought. The point that I want to make is that all we have to do is to look around and we will see that just about everyone is driven *not* to be alone, in a generalized sense. Token contact with others is sought compulsively, while at the same time the capacity to relate more deeply is stunted. Outside stimulation, preferably loud and manic, seems to be a must. Car radios must be blaring; one must text or use one's cell phone constantly while driving, even though it is illegal and demonstrably dangerous; stores must have music or blaring television sets; people must be on their cell phones almost constantly, even when dining together, even when walking on the street, or in the woods; kids and many adults must turn on their radios, start to play video games or call someone almost as soon as they are alone. Addicts of all stripes use this kind of outside distraction to try to avoid becoming aware of their inner lives. Once again we have a ubiquitous symptom of significant pathology, a basic dread of solitude with the self, that is rarely perceived as such, or whose manifestations are seen at best as relatively innocuous, certainly normal in both the clinical and statistical sense. Who would take this ubiquitous behavior by normal people as pathological? Who would go to see a psychiatrist because they need to be on the phone constantly? Nevermind that this inability to be alone points to severe psychological impoverishment and alienation, if not worse. Since 'everybody does it', since it is the norm, it must be 'normal' and thus cannot be pathological. Pointing this phenomenon out and calling it symptomatic of severe pathology is likely to be seen as a gross exaggeration, a therapist's making a lot of fuss about nothing. The behavior is entirely 'normal' – in the mathematical sense. It is normal in a clinical sense only if we accept a statistical criterion of mental health.[52]

The second example regarding the pathological self concerns how we see our 'inner lives'. It is another reflection of our dualistic view. The developmental version of pathology that I have been presenting revolves around the mechanized splitting of the fundamental unity of our being, of the holistic state that I have proposed characterizes each person's entry into this world and continues to invisibly underlie all of our subsequent experiences. (I believe that this unitary way of being was probably much more of a living presence in life under p-orality – a possibility that I will consider in chapters 7 and 8.) I have said a number of times that in response to our madness this ineffable state condenses into three major solid, apparently autonomous, separable, unconnected entities: language, self and world. Furthermore, although so far I haven't emphasized it, I have mentioned the problematic relationship between that self and world that follows from this disruptive partitioning. Thinking about self and world in these bifurcating ways automatically leads to the perennial problems and paradoxes about perception, thought, cognition, meaning, reference, inner phenomena, other minds, reality and antireality, and so on.[53]

I want to comment briefly on the madness of our 'perceptions of the inner' – meaning, roughly, what it is that we all believe we see when we look inside ourselves, at what we take as internally generated: thoughts, feelings, chatter, wishes, fears, loves, pains – or rather, 'referents' of these terms, the 'object-like entities' to which these words presumably refer, their meanings (thus raising, among other paradoxes, the conundrum of what it is that we think we see that we have not generated ourselves – the outside world? – and what it means). We automatically accept the incoherent notion of an internal observer who is observing all sorts of phenomena. Supposedly some of these impressions come from the inside, others from the outside. What is the relationship between 'us' (ourselves, the ego, the 'I', subject) and the internal phenomena this self (thinks it) observes? This is the model taken seriously by almost all psychotherapists, psychiatrists and other physicians, psychologists, philosophers, students of consciousness (unless they just reductively ignore the phenomenon of awareness). This picture of humans' inner life is accepted without question, and is widely used in one way or another by all disciplines that involve human behavior and consciousness in any way, and that includes just about all of them. (The presence of this picture in a discipline such as mathematics is not easy to see, but it is there.)[54] Yet it is a bogus model generated by our mad dichotomizing and abstracting. It would not be possible unless we all were little twinned Douglases. Even these brief considerations give us a glimpse of just how far-reaching and pervasive the manifestations of humanity's madness are.

Incidentally, I believe that the mental health disciplines ought to take seriously the later Wittgenstein's enigmatic comments about these standard pictures of language and inner objects – for example, his difficult remarks about the untenability of the idea of a private language.[55] I believe that they are highly relevant to these fields, even though they were meant for philosophers. He frequently, but often indirectly, refers to the folly of conceptualizing an inner world populated by object-like entities that can be referred to by words or terms. As pointed out earlier, Wittgenstein does not offer solutions to the kinds of paradox raised by the notion of, say, pain, or of rule-following. Instead he just states traditional alternative positions, shows that they are untenable (for philosophers) and leaves it at that. If I read him correctly, his position is that philosophy and philosophers need to settle for and act on the view that, in language, 'nothing extraordinary is involved', that all we need to understand about it 'already lies open to view',[56] that philosophers ought to work at the level of ordinary, everyday use and clarify problems pertaining to that use. In a way, this echoes Heidegger's phenomenological method that assumes that we humans can investigate our own kind of being by investigating our supposedly innate understanding of that being.[57] Wittgenstein does, however, show us what is wrong with the normal pictures, and that ought to give pause to psychiatrists, psychoanalysts, clinical psychologists and other mental health practitioners.[58]

As a therapist, I consider this paradox of the inner to be critical. Wittgenstein was aware of the limitations of this formalistic, referential model of the person, perhaps because his engineering training and experience made him aware of the conceptual limitations of the framework that I call the state process formalism. I previously cited one of his insightful and salient remarks, but they are worth repeating in the present context:

> How does the philosophical problem about mental processes and states and about behaviorism arise? – The first step is the one that altogether escapes notice. We talk of processes and states and leave their nature undecided. Sometime perhaps we shall know more about them – we think. But that is just what commits us to a particular way of looking at this matter. For we have a definite concept of what it means to know a process better. (The decisive movement in the conjuring trick has been made, and it is the very one that we thought quite innocent.)[59]

(The problems that arise from this usage certainly are not, or should not be, problems just for philosophers.) Unfortunately, his critique seems to have fallen on deaf ears. I haven't seen it discussed, either in philosophy or in the mental health disciplines.[60] State process formalisms continue to be the unacknowledged, covert and ubiquitous models in the human disciplines. The incoherences that they raise remain out of sight. As far as I am concerned, the critiques of the picture that I have just discussed call into question just about everything that the mental health professions (and perhaps other disciplines as well) believe and practice. The view of humanity's madness that I have been sketching calls for entirely different remedial approaches, values and perspectives. For example, just about all familiar therapeutic goals involving changes to the self – such as raising self-esteem, allaying symptoms of anxiety, removing distortions about reality, getting in touch with the real self and so on – are rooted in a mad worldview: the spectator view of interior and exterior grounded in the received view of language. (I don't expect this view to be welcomed by most colleagues.) To ground therapy approaches in this model seems questionable at best.

One could continue giving examples of symptomatic manifestations of humanity's madness *ad infinitum*. For example, symptoms can be identified in our attitudes, behaviors and beliefs about sports, health, food, mental health, medicine, crime, competition, cars, government and on and on. I hope that the preparatory work about language, self and world that laid the foundation for the above examples of madness' symptoms gives at least an inkling of what I see as a hugely disabling condition of our lives: the roots of our misperceptions of reality that tacitly but devastatingly thwart our attempts to deal with the global threats that we are facing – and much more.

Now what?

An awareness of the nature and consequences of our pervasive 'normal' madness leads to two obvious questions and problems. First, if indeed we are mad, what might sanity be like? Can a mad world even imagine, let alone move toward, a saner way of being in the world? (Can literates imagine p-orality?) And, second, even if we can and actually do sketch a viable, realistic vision of sanity, what then? How might humanity move away from being mad? How can we deal successfully with the rabid defenses that are stirred up if and when one attempts to ameliorate that madness (or, for that matter, any pathology)? Who is sane enough to initiate such a mission? Chapters 7 and 8 offer parting thoughts on these baffling questions.

7
Visions of Sanity

Madness and sanity

How can we begin to understand the sanity/madness polarity and its closely related twin, mental health/mental illness? It is a subject that has confounded the mental health disciplines, although they haven't advertised the fact. (It is ironic that the issue is foreshadowed by the subject area's very name.) A simple approach, and one that therefore is usually followed, is to extend general medicine's standard views about health and illness to the psychological realm. By and large, each of these pairs is seen as complementary, mutually exclusive and jointly exhaustive. Having more of one of them means having less of the other. You are healthy to the extent that you aren't sick, sane to the extent that you aren't mad, psychologically healthy to the extent that you aren't mentally ill. If only things were that simple.

Recently, an unorthodox and singularly insightful monograph appeared that is devoted to exploring just these kinds of issue. Its title states the author's basic premise, and suggests the problem: *Normality Does Not Equal Mental Health: The Need to Look Elsewhere for Standards of Good Psychological Health*. Here are the opening sentences of the first chapter:

> Psychological normality has remained one of the last as well as one of the most central unexamined presuppositions of current psychiatry and clinical psychology. With few exceptions in the literature, psychological normality has served as an unquestioned standard of mental health while the same standard has been used to equate deviations from normality with mental illness.[1]

The psychologist-philosopher author Steven Bartlett has a great deal to say about this difficult and problematic subject area, but by and large his orientation and perspective differ considerably from the ones that I am unfolding. A major difference is that the two developmental landmarks that are the primary conceptual and experiential ingredients in my approach play no role in his. However, Bartlett's book shows just how complicated the issues are Their comprehensive exploration is far beyond the scope of the present work; what I will say about sanity will necessarily be sketchy, and reflect the limited nature of the goals that I am pursuing.

Within that developmentally illuminated conception of madness, what can be said about madness' other, the state or condition we call sanity? As Bartlett's opening comments imply, anyone hoping to find a promising start in the psychiatric literature will be disappointed. Virtually all mainstream journal articles and textbooks that I have examined that deal with the subject of mental health echo his point. Most begin by stating that the pathology/health dyad is complex, controversial, problematic, puzzling and that no clear answers are forthcoming.[2] Numerous alternative conceptions have been offered, but none seems satisfactory. One book review of an early monograph on the subject, a textbook that was, and still is, considered to be authoritative, begins by saying that

> Purchasers will probably be disappointed if they expect to find much that is of direct value to rehabilitation or that contributes in a substantive way to the founding of a new science of normality.[3]

Because it is an appealingly simple solution, 'mental health' and normalcy are conflated – the basic belief that Bartlett calls into question. When examined more closely it becomes obvious that both concepts are nebulous. Is normalcy statistical, clinical or prognostic?[4] Is, or should, the criterion be mental health be medical, sociocultural, political, economic, humanistic, psychodynamic, behavioral, ethical-moral or a combination of some or all of these? Is mental health absolute or relative? Is it, or should it be, the same all over the world, or does it/should it vary from culture to culture? Is it defined by the absence of debilitating symptoms or, alternatively, by the presence of sanctioned, admired abilities, prized 'mental faculties', lofty experiences, talents? How do the contemporary and specifically local views about ontology and epistemology affect one's conception? Who is to set the criteria?

The confusion about this pair was already evident decades ago, and it continues unabated. Allen Frances, the chair of the taskforce that produced the version of psychiatry's biblical *Diagnostic and Statistical Manual of Mental Disorders* that preceded the current new version, stated that 'Fads punctuate what has become a basic background of over-diagnosis. Normality is an endangered species.'[5] Frances identifies eight contributing factors, including ease of meeting diagnostic criteria, pressures from the pharmaceutical industry, media hype and widespread lack of tolerance for even relatively minor discomforts. The old text mentioned earlier identified four concepts of normality: absence of pathology; reaching a quasi-mystical ideal of self-actualization; statistical, just average; and transactional (good interplay between inner and interpersonal group experience).[6] Bartlett believes that

> The defining characteristics of good mental health include such characteristics as consciousness of high values and dedication to ends that have intrinsic value, heightened perceptual abilities, creativity, aesthetic sensibility and greater responsiveness to beauty, resistance to enculturation and resulting conformity, and what I have elsewhere referred to as moral intelligence.[7]

Radical alternatives

Now what do all of these visions of health and illness have in common? From the point of view advanced in the preceding chapters, it is that all of these conceptions are unwittingly grounded in orthodox received views. When we look more closely at any or all of these kinds of conception of health or normality we can identify the presence of symptoms and characteristics of the coupled received views of self, language and world: the implicit reliance on reified concepts or other abstractions, the readiness to detach and separate, depersonalize; the inevitable rash of dualisms; the abstractions that have been taken for realities; the ubiquitous presence of the separability assumption. We remain in the familiar Cartesian-Newtonian worldview, in familiar epistemological and ontological dualistic, separatist, fragmenting, reality-distorting paradoxical frameworks and presuppositions no matter which of the usual views of normality and pathology we employ. Therefore, from the perspective that has been developed here, one must expect all of the concepts to be seriously restrictive, misleading, madness-generating and supporting, retaining the mad distortions of reality.

What I have tried to do in the preceding chapters is to set the stage for a radically alternative general ontological/epistemological framework grounded in hypotheses about neonates' acquisition of their first language and humanity's acquisition of literacy. The proposed conceptions included the neonate's ineffable state, an equally ineffable step into the linguistic dimension, the glimpse of language as part of a baffling unity that includes self and world, a holistic way of being (p-orality) that precipitates into literacy's polarized, categorizing, separatist, referential, hyper-rational logic and cognition-dominated world. The framework also included the speculation that p-orality was a pretheorizing, prethematizing quasi-unitary way of being in the world – *quasi*-unitary because p-orals can be presumed to have had a tacit grasp of real differences, an unspoken sense that there are some boundaries. Thus, under my presuppositions that grasp does not consist of abstract, articulated assumptions about inside and outside. Rather, it is an unreflective and unreflexive near-unitary competence to deal with the demands of life, having a realistic mature understanding of being in the world, but one that is not tied to distorting formalizing and cognizing abstractions (definitions, analyses, boundarying), to constant reifying, self-referring, of taking signifieds as real, objectifying self and language, defining and quantifying everything in sight, predicating, relying on underlying state process formalisms and on and on. That *via negativa* specification (positing that sanity is none of these) begins to outline my model of sanity, adumbrating an ineffable unitary way of being. I propose that this unitary state can give us a glimpse of what 'mental health' ought to be. It is not consciousness raising, not raising self-esteem, not overcoming anxiety or other psychiatric symptoms.

As I have noted at several junctures, I see much of the radical, almost incomprehensible efforts of major radical thinkers, especially Heidegger, Wittgenstein, Derrida and Merleau Ponty, as attempts to move in this direction (both Wittgenstein and Heidegger avoided positing any philosophical theory of language).[8] I believe that these attempts were only partially successful and, as I have said before, see their shortcomings as the inevitable consequence of limits entailed by these thinkers' failure to consider the developmental dimension in any depth. Lacking this conceptual resource, they necessarily remained locked in Cartesian dualism. For example, Heidegger struggled mightily to evolve a totally different view of language. This is exemplified in his obscure ideas about prereflective, prereflexive, prephenomenological, pre-ontological, pretheoretical thinking, poiesis, a holistic prepredicative understanding. It shows in his emphasis on the contrast between the apophantic and the hermeneutic 'as': the apophantic 'as' asserts; it lets something be seen as something else; it is a predication: 'Truth is…"X"'; 'the cat is on the mat'. Furthermore, Heidegger reversed the usual causal picture of language as something that originates in persons, making language the originating house of being instead. That might be a radical, even quasi-mystical, proposition but it only reverses figure and ground, the direction of origins. It still maintains the basic language-self dualism, both parts of a separatist dichotomy, and thus is not a unitary, non-dual alternative. Nevertheless, I see Heidegger as having an intuitive holistic sense of language. For example, the philosopher Wayne Owens tells us that he believed 'that the nature of language qualifies as what can be called a mystery, and ... that anything said about language should be taken as no more than a wave on the mysterious ocean of language itself'.[9] We also know about his interest in Zen thought.

Yet, in spite of Heidegger's intent, to the unwary reader at least, much of what he said about language in numerous works does strongly suggest that, to him, language did unwittingly remain an entity of sorts: he says that it is a 'something' that gets a grip on the world; reveals itself, its essence; is something that we can be 'brought to': can appear to us; comes to presence; is a primal phenomenon; has an essential nature; can withdraw; is and remains the master of man; and so forth. Heidegger also implicitly relies on a Cartesian ontology when he talks about something unspoken that remains in 'mind'; refers to phenomenology, to persons having experiences, and thus as observing inner events; to an unfolding of or relating to 'language as language', implying a reification; a 'showing within', implying an inner-outer dualism; when he speaks of a personal experience one can undergo with language, he constantly refers to mind, thinking.[10] Thus it is difficult to avoid the conclusion that in spite of his best intentions and avowed non-dual goals, the ways in which Heidegger discusses many issues about language illustrates that although he may very well have denied it, without realizing it he still saw the world in basically Cartesian, bifurcating, objectifying terms – perhaps unavoidably so, bound as we all are by the subject-predicate, thing-attribute structure of language. As I have said, he refers to an observer to whom things appear, who has thoughts, a mind. He still strongly implies a separatist conception of language – it remains a 'something' that can be identified, thought about, given to us, and is distinguishable from the human being (Dasein). It must be acknowledged, though, that Heidegger did struggle in various ways to try to get away from the formalist restrictions imposed on us all by language – or, at least, by our received view. He crossed out words, invented new ones, waxed poetic. In Wittgenstein's case, the attempt to get away from a separatist view of language shows in the pragmatic stance of his later work. He refused to consider language as an object of study, something that could be isolated. Instead, he insisted on dealing with language only in context, in use (language games, forms of life).

Both thinkers' positions are complicated and all too often obscure, but both did eschew the normal, traditional kind of theorizing about language.[11] I believe that both Heidegger and Wittgenstein had a sense that any theorizing 'of the normal kind' about language – that is, theorizing that would ape the natural sciences' formalistic-logical model of theorizing and empirical study – would necessarily miss that which is central to languaging. In a complex and obscure fashion, Heidegger and Wittgenstein shared an aversion to such practices. Richard Rorty commented on this commonality:

> On my reading of them, then, these two great philosophers passed each other in mid-career, going in opposite directions. Wittgenstein, in the *Tractatus*, started from a point which, to a pragmatist like myself, seems much less enlightened than that of *Being and Time*. But, as Wittgenstein advanced in the direction of pragmatism, he met Heidegger coming the other way – retreating from pragmatism into the same escapist mood in which the *Tractatus* had been written, attempting to regain in 'thought' the sort of sublimity which the young Wittgenstein had found in logic.[12]

Michael Polanyi's notion of tacit knowledge mentioned in Chapter 3 also seems close to non-dual thought. I believe that yet another allusion to this modality can be discerned in Wittgenstein's remark pertaining to that which distinguishes certainty from formal propositional knowledge: "something animal as it were".[13] This kind of thinking beclouds the subject-predicate distinction and tends to displace thematizing. I believe that a case can even be made that Derrida points to a non-dual vision of language when he claims that terms do not have non-linguistic referents or signifieds, that all is text, that the signifiers only signify more signifiers.

The two developmental roots of sanity

What, then, might be an alternative view of sanity, normality, 'mental health' that follows from the complex dual developmental framework that I have been sketching? One way of conceptualizing it is from a linguistic perspective. We have considered the ontogenetic and the phylogenetic aspects of development. Each contributes one way of conceptualizing non-dual sanity. The ontogenetic perspective is grounded in the hypotheses about the neonate state, hatching and maturation. As I conceive it, at birth the infant's view of the world is, if not sane, at least not mad. If that is so, then with hatching, the step into the linguistic dimension, conceivably that sane-like state could continue if the mad environment didn't deflect it and create the twinned little Douglases. I am suggesting that a language user may be a language *user*, yet also have a drastically different view of language, a view totally unlike the received view – really, no view at all, a "no-view". We then would have a sane young child that had not been infected by adults' bifurcating madness. It would have a non- or atheoretical, unthematized relationship with language, linked to a particular non-dual, non-thematizing, non-reflective/reflexive way of having a self, world and language. Talking and listening would be on the order of breathing and other unthematized aspects of being, the kind of languaging that I believe Heidegger and company were struggling to depict. To the degree that such a child had remained unspoiled by gratuitous abstracting and abstractions, formalizing, defining, fragmenting, boundarying and dichotomizing, abstracting would be minimal and relatively innocuous. Such a child would not cognize language, yet still would be very much in touch with reality, dealing with their world competently in an integrated, attuned fashion.

We next turn to the other developmental perspective, the phylogenetic one. The kind of 'theory-less' (non-)view of language use that I am attempting to describe is not only exemplified by the post-hatched child's way of being but also resonates with phylogenetic speculations about the p-oral state. My idea is that, in this state, most of the time, language use would happen unselfconsciously, as it were pretheoretically, without explicit, deliberate cognitive activity, in much the same way that I described the young child's early languaging. P-orals would just talk and listen – a state just about unimaginable to us mad literates, people who inevitably and necessarily see reading and writing and referring everywhere, lurking behind all manifestations of language – actually, behind and under manifestations of anything and everything, behind and under our perceptions and conceptions. That is, my guess is that p-orals' languaging is a 'use' of language that once again, just as in the case of the child, is not at all a use of language per se. Language would not have been regarded as a tool, although to the outside, literacy-tainted observer the p-orals' uncorrupted-by-madness kind of languaging would almost certainly be perceived as normal tool use of a semiotic system. (Everett's perception of the Pirahãs' use of language is an example.)

This impossibility of comprehending this drastic alternative possibility parallels our inability to understand the neonatal state. We cannot imagine a way of speaking and listening that isn't separatist (in Roy Harris's sense – see chapter 2), where language isn't taken as a separate tool, a foreign object. I am convinced that these two envisioned radical modes of languaging – the neonate's prelinguistic state and the p-oral's a-literate state – can be specified only negatively, in the same manner in which Wittgenstein 'described' that about which one must remain silent. All we can say about that conception of language is what it is not. These speculations point toward what I see as a non-dual way of being in the world.

Elementary sanity evolves

I have been sketching two ideal conditions of sanity, two different but ontologically and epistemologically related hypothetical unitary ways of being a self in a world: the neonates' and the p-orals' states that are conceptualized as non-dual, non-fragmented, integrated, undifferentiated, at one with nature and with reality, not planned yet adequate, competent. I next want to modify these pure ideals to bring them down to earth, to make them less alien. I want to add the following qualifier: sanity, our madness' other, is the condition, the way of being, that is as unitary as possible – an equivocal, ambiguous modification. That is, the ideal non-dual ineffable state is not the only one employed. The modification says that this way of being is unlikely to be the only mode of existence, to be adequate across the board. There almost certainly would have been times and situations in the course of the p-orals' seamless non-dual existences when some changing circumstances in self and world would have called for a shift to reflection, abstraction, to a structuring, quasi-abstract way of being that foreshadows our mad state. The same could be said about the young child's way of being in the world. There would have been moments of rudimentary abstracting in response to atypical demands. In other words, I am hypothesizing that people living in a unitary state, young children and p-orals both would occasionally encounter some problem or situation that called for more than their normal unselfconscious, unthematizing and adequate coping responses. Under some pressures they would have to modify their usual and usually near-automatic, successful ways of dealing with tasks in ways that are reminiscent of Polanyi's descriptions of tacit knowledge at work. In other words, there would have been some specific circumstances that realistically demanded going beyond just doing, just being, coping unreflectively, without analysis, without adopting the separatist, distanced and distancing, calculating and 'objective' observer's stance.

In Taylor's terminology, situations would arise that necessitated some degree of appropriate disengagement, a stepping back, reflecting. At that point, for the moment there would be a shift. The non-dually existing individuals' ways of being in the world would temporarily have become more like the ways of the literacy-surrounded mad successors.

That proposal raises key questions: What would be a 'realistic' demand? When would a normally non-dual person truly, 'realistically' need to move into an abstracting, formalizing, unity-destroying mode? Mad humanity would not formulate this question. It would not arise, since humankind sees its mode of being as sane. Here we have an example of the kinds of benefits that a *via negativa* can yield. Here the negative definition of a non-dual way of being has raised a question that as far as I know is novel. In our abstracting way of life, how often is the question of whether abstracting is called for raised? How often do we stop and examine whether our normal cognitive-abstracting, computer-oriented methods are appropriate, realistic, productive? Is it not possible, then, that this is exactly what has been wrong with humanity's approaches to major global problems, what accounts for their failures – that we have been unable to step back and try to see, understand, whether the standard abstracting, objectifying (mad) approach to problem-solving is really called for, is appropriate, in a particular instance? And whether in a given situation turning decision-making to computers is sane, or whether it is inappropriate, highly dangerous, driven by a fatal distortion of reality? By the way, I fully realize that the conception that I am proposing involves circular reasoning: reality is what demands the step out of non-duality; non-duality needs to be discarded when reality demands that. Reality has not been pinned down. So be it.

But – and here is the other major element of my conception of sanity – having had such an encounter with a problem or situation that did demand a temporary shift into near-madness, then after that shift. When it is no longer appropriate, it is crucial that persons return to their previous unreflective, engaged stance toward the world. The fluid, unthematized, unitary, prereflective way of being in the world needs to return automatically. It ought to be the norm, the default position, not the artist's or mystic's exceptional state. The thematization, disengagement, abstracting, distancing ought to be only temporary, ought to last only as long as needed, and no longer. To me, that is what being attuned to reality means. The flexible, appropriate back-and-forth movement between the two modes of being would reflect the demands of 'the really real'. That reality is impossible to define, but appears and has its impact, provided one is not locked into insane, inflexible abstracting of everything. (Informally one might say that reality is that which if ignored will come back to haunt us.)

Under this view, then, humanity's current madness can be seen as a kind of rigidity, an inability to move in and out of the abstracting mode, a near-total estrangement from its other, the near-unitary state. At this point, humanity seems incapable of reversing its historical move-ment into abstraction, the evolution that in our civilization is repeated in most infants' way of hatching. We are stuck in only one of what ought to be only one of two mutually supportive, appropriately fluc-tuating states. Madness means being trapped, ossified, unable to return to sane fluidity. As a matter of fact, in our rigidity we have come to see any drastic alternative to our sciencing, technologizing, objectify-ing approaches to solving problems as weakness, a failure of logic and rigor – ironically, a loss of 'objectivity'. And this rigidity suggests that there are most likely many situations in which formalizing, dehumaniz-ing dualism is not only inappropriate but greatly distorts reality – is mad, dangerous, destructive. (It is interesting and suggestive that Heidegger speaks of language as revealing but also as withdrawing, showing and concealing.)

A contemporary model

To me, recent chronicles and discussions by anthropologists, linguists and missionaries about the strange Pirahã Amazon tribe suggest that this tribe has retained important residues of a p-oral way of life and that its ways are sane. The tribe's sanity is suggested by a number of its qualities, including its accurate attunement to its environment and its superb abil-ity to cope. It is unlike the impoverished groups of illiterates that Ong and others offered as near-models of p-orality. This tribe as a whole, and its individual members, are exceedingly competent, doing very well in a very dangerous environment, and seem remarkably free of what we call 'mental illness'. Dan Everett, the linguist and ex-missionary whose work with the Pirahãs was mentioned in Chapter 2, finds no signs of depression, chronic fatigue, extreme anxiety, panic attacks or other psy-chological ailments that are common in many industrialized societies. They do not even have a word for 'worry.' Antisocial acts are extremely rare. Children function well (see below and Chapter 8). Everett empha-sizes that the tribe does so well not because its life is simple, primitive, or lacks pressures. The tribe as a whole and its individual members are doing very well in a very dangerous environment:

Pirahãs laugh about everything. They laugh at their own misfortune: when someone's hut blows over in a rainstorm, the occupants laugh more loudly than anyone. They laugh when they catch a lot of fish. They laugh when they catch no fish. They laugh when they're full and they laugh when they're hungry... This pervasive happiness is hard to explain, though I believe that the Pirahãs are so confident and secure in their ability to handle anything that their environment throws at them that they can enjoy whatever comes their way. This is not at all because their lives are easy, but because they are good at what they do.[14]

This is a further characteristic that suggests that sanity is their militant resistance to abstracting, or adopting literacy's distortions in general: The Pirahãs value direct experience and observation highly. They live according to what Everett calls 'the immediacy of experience principle': 'Formulaic language and actions (rituals) that involve reference to no witnesses events are avoided'.[15] Their thinking doesn't fit into our logical molds. For example, they refuse to complete syllogisms because in terms of an individual's concrete experience these are meaningless, incoherent, gratuitous. Psychologists and linguists who have attempted to study them have been hugely frustrated. Their Pirahã 'subjects' view such efforts with good-natured amusement, play along (because they are paid), but refuse to indulge in what they consider to be empty, useless kinds of reasoning.[16]

These kinds of abstraction-resisting responses and attitudes are very much like those encountered by Luria in his field studies of illiterate as well as somewhat literate persons in the remoter areas of Uzbekistan, except that in the Pirahã case the refusals to go along with Western ways and expectations seem to have an underlay of making fun of the investigators.[17] When tested, Luria's subjects referred to geometrical figures by identifying them with familiar objects (plates, doors) rather than in abstract terms. In tests designed to test the categorization of a group of objects, persons grouped these according to their roles in practical situations, common use; test subjects evinced 'situational thinking', actively resisting classifying them, putting them in categories. One group had names only for objects that were useful in their lives, giving the rest a generalized label. What to us is normal cognitive activity is rejected across the board. For example, when asked to respond to the syllogism 'in a certain place ['X'], all bears are white ... ['X'] is a place where there always is snow. What is the color of the bears in

['X']?', one subject's response was 'I don't know. I've seen a black bear. I've never seen any others.' You find out about a bear's color by looking, not reasoning about it. When asked to define 'tree', one subject said: 'Why should I [define what a tree is]? Everyone knows what a tree is; they don't need me telling them.' Reading Everett's description of the experimental efforts of his colleagues, one gets a sense that in the Pirahãs' case, their non-responsiveness is much more sophisticated, ironic, playful than that. They are having fun with the scholars.

One of the abstractions excluded by the Pirahãs' immediacy of experience principle is religion. Very properly, Everett was unable to claim that he had direct contact with the originators of his religion. If one lacks direct supporting evidence, a story isn't believed. It simply becomes irrelevant. So his stories did not impress the Pirahã. They explicitly told Everett that they liked him and so would welcome his continued stay, but only on condition that he stopped proselytizing. Eventually, in spite of his missionary's strong and longstanding religious beliefs, Everett found their way of life so compelling, even irresistible, that it changed his life. Although he started his work as a missionary and linguist, in the course of his four decades of living with the Pirahã, studying their language and customs, he became an atheist. He ends his book with this striking statement: 'The Pirahãs are an unusually happy and contented people. I would go so far as to suggest that the Pirahãs are happier, fitter, and better adjusted to their environment than any Christian or other religious person I have ever known.'[18]

Everett says little about his observations of the Pirahãs' inner life. He gives no indication that he expected it to be any different in principle from the kind that is taken for granted in the typical Western person. Although he doesn't say so explicitly, the way in which Everett talks about his observations strongly suggests that he doesn't question this sameness: for him the Pirahã can be expected to have the same kinds of thoughts, wishes, ideas, concepts, definitions of words, grammar, rigid boundaries (self/other, inside/outside and so on) as we have. They can be expected to 'observe their inner lives, and report on them'. So, to see beyond Everett's descriptions one has to try to read between the lines. If one does, one can find hints here and there of something different, alien, in the Pirahã's way of being in the world. For example, the naming of a person is flexible. The name might be changed over the course of the person's life, suggesting a certain absence of sedimentation, of rigid abstraction. My guess is that the Pirahã's theory of the self is much like Heidegger's theory of language: there isn't any. That, however, is the sort of conjecture about p-orality, which was discussed in Chapter 4, that because of its very nature can be neither confirmed nor disconfirmed. As I have indicated numerous times by now, my guess is that a non-dual way of life includes a non-reflexive, one could say 'thought-less', condition of the self (and language, and world). That way of being would not raise any explicit concern or thought about abstractions and philosophical puzzles such as intelligence, values, pains, wishes, hostility, love, reality, wordless thought, self-referential sentences. The Pirahã probably have no conception of language as a separate entity, and thus no explicit conception of naming, referring, definitions and so on. Much of the time, languaging would be just a matter of living unself-consciously in a unitary self-language-world constellation. Still, probably they also have something vaguely like latent, incipient definitions: they could explain what their words or sentences meant, and did so to Everett – if and when asked. Aristotle thought that humans are creatures who by their nature desire to know, but I believe this is true just of mad Westernized people who for millennia have been swimming in a literary, reality-distorting abstracting ocean. I see the Pirahã's sanity is just to be, to be effective, competent, attuned to and responsive to nature – without nuclear weapons, investment accounts, football teams, cell phones.

I see these and similar considerations as having considerable relevance for our conception of therapy and health. They ought to be food for thought for mental health professionals.

It bears repeating that the exotic and paradoxical aspects of a non-dual state are such that active questioning and external observations by dualistically oriented persons simply cannot reveal such a unitary condition. As I have noted in several contexts by now, nonduality flees, necessarily goes into hiding, as soon as one attempts to investigate it. Observation by 'non-non-duals' precipitates formalization – a sort of quantum-mechanics-like observer effect: on observation, a probability function condenses into a datum. Likewise, any answers to questions about non-dual experience necessarily mean that the responder has already abandoned the non-dual condition in order to comply. The previously nondualistically oriented observer now needs to deliberately observe – describe, report, objectify, formalize in terms of our subject-predicate, object-attribute grammar. In response to formalizing questions, the previously unitary person has become the self-referential, reflexive fragmented observer-observed dyad.

I have been sketching a conception of sanity – nebulous, unscientific, unsupported by empirical data. I have also claimed that the very nature of nonduality makes it virtually impossible to formalize it, to gather evidence about it that will conform to standards of scientific rigor. I suppose the credibility of these conjectures and pictures will depend on one's constellation of beliefs and the attendant psychological makeup. In any case, though, whether or not one finds the above hypotheses and arguments credible or interesting, there remains the seriously vexing and pressing question of what can be done about the hazardous state of our world, the question that motivated this work.

I have outlined an alternative to what I have characterized as our mad state: a mutable shifting between unitary and bifurcating, cognizing modes in response to the demands of reality. The thesis is that seeing the world's dangers from this flexible and realistic perspective could, and hopefully would, allow the evolution of new and productive understanding of our problems that will point us toward effective remedial approaches. The obvious question that has been lurking in the background all along is how, then, is that to be done?

Chapter 8 will outline some approaches that seem to me to follow on from the conception of sanity developed here. However, at any one time one can see only so far. For me, the evolution of thought and insights has always been an onion layer peeling process. The views that I offer are, can only be, those that have evolved up to this point and become available. Some insights even have come to light only in the course of writing this book (my usual experience). Thus, this work is only a way station. I do not see it as offering definitive, conclusive views or solutions. The recommendations in Chapter 8 are transitional, provisional. Perhaps the best I can hope for is that they will provide a starting point for further onion-peeling by others. As Wittgenstein says toward the end of the Preface to his *Philosophical Investigations*, 'I should not like my writing to spare other people the trouble of thinking. But, if possible, to stimulate someone to thoughts of his own.'

8
Toward Restorative Change

We know the solution

Before I offer some ideas that emerged from the preceding hypotheses and discussions, I want to get a few issues out of the way. Let us remember the fundamental hypothesis framed at the very beginning of this book. I proposed that as seen from inside the framework of our usual Western abstraction- and cognition-dominated dualistic worldview, from the one-sided and essentially still Cartesian mind-body, word-thing, inner-outer perspective, without realizing it we are severely constricted in the kinds of 'solution' that we can conceptualize. We cannot imagine, or even consider, the possibility that one could address our current disastrously dangerous situation in any but our received-views dominated ways – which means scientistically, hyper-rationally, in terms of normal science's standard framework and presuppositions. Yes, there are some faint voices calling for 'spiritual' changes – humanity's awakening, a shift to a semimystical new age position, a wholesale religious or economic upheaval, a return to some earlier golden age – but these are drowned out by the din of activities and proposals that continue to be rooted in the standard enframing, science/technology perspective, supplemented by strident defensive denials that insist that there are no real dangers, that global threats are nefariously motivated myths, that what we need and must concentrate on is producing more jobs, lowering taxes, strengthening our military, reducing government control and aid to the needy, and so on. At any rate, the hope that some global consciousness-raising is imminent and will save us does not seem promising to me.

The scientism-driven refrain is that science/technology can solve all, that we know all about our difficulties and how to solve them. Some say that we are already doing so, even doing too much. Others maintain that we could be solving all pressing problems if only the efforts were not being stymied by opposing forces. These matters raise many questions and issues, but I want to focus on the topic of science's neutrality that was touched on in chapters 1 and 6.[1] The story goes that science indeed is neutral, everyone knows it is,[2] it can be used for good or evil, and that's the end of it. But that is not quite the whole story: The scientist

> may be aware of real ethical and political problems, but these occur only after the facts of the hard science. The atom is 'split' and later comes the moral quandary over the use of nuclear weapons.[3]

> This division allows science to retain its authority. In spite of what may happen in the outside world, the scientist can still be convinced he is on the one true path to truth, complete truth. Any shortcomings of science when it is brought into contact with the world arise because the truth is as yet inadequate, incomplete.

> And the division between scientific knowledge and the world produces a cast-iron moral defence. The question of whether to employ the atom bomb, the scientist will argue, is precisely the same as the question of whether one uses a gun...Nothing has changed except the effectiveness of the tools, the scale of the possible error.[4]

That science is neutral is a highly appealing view, and history shows that questioning it raises emotional, intense defensive responses.[5] The debates continue:

Suzuki

> The machine, behaviorism, the conditioned reflex, Communism, artificial insemination, automation generally, vivisection, the H-bomb – they are, each and all, most intimately related, and form close-welded solid links of a logical chain...The sciences are uniformly centrifugal, extroverted, and they look 'objectively' toward the thing they pick up for study. The position they thus assume is to keep the thing away from them and never to strive to identify themselves with the object of their study. Even when they look within for self-inspection they are careful to project outwardly what is within, thus making themselves foreign to themselves as if what is within did not belong to them. They are utterly afraid of being 'subjective.' Scientific knowledge of the Self is not real knowledge as long as it objectifies the Self.[6]

Appleyard (3, 4 + 6)

7, 7

8, 13

I believe that numerous deeper thinkers have concluded that science is not at all neutral, that it is 'not a neutral or innocent commodity which can be employed as a convenience by people wishing to partake only of the West's material power. Rather it is spiritually corrosive... It cannot really co-exist with anything.'[7] Science has a concealed ethic. It dominates, puts nature to the rack, insists on public, repeatable verification, believes in truth and an autonomous reality, demands quantification and formalist reasoning, exiles everything that isn't 'objective' – and is full of unrecognized, or perhaps disavowed, presuppositions. It is a covert metaphysics – in Heidegger's framework, it becomes the current version of ontotheology. These kinds of view, although they contradict the commonsense and consensual benign-neutrality view, ought to be taken very seriously, listened to, examined carefully. The vast majority of people, though, are likely to see them as eccentric, bizarre, ignoring the obvious realities.

Virulent debates about this issue continue,[8] but they seem curiously unbalanced. I am referring to the same kind of asymmetry that obtained between Herder and Condillac that was discussed in Chapter 3. One side – almost always the radical, more revolutionary one – is perfectly able to understand the other's traditional, mainstream position and reasoning, but the reverse is not true. The traditionalists often know but little about the opposing unorthodox views. They see no point in even studying them since they must be so obviously wrong. All too often the traditionalists know just enough about these to be able to misrepresent and disdainfully them. On the other hand, the radicals – here, those who say that science is not neutral – the critics of scientism ('the belief that science is or can be the complete and only explanation'),[9] usually not only know a good deal about science – many have been, or still are, scientists – but also about philosophy Thus they do know and understand the traditional pro-science arguments made by their opponents, the advocates of scientism and scientific neutrality. However, since they are also familiar with unorthodox philosophical thought, they also see grave problems in orthodox science's mostly unexamined and unquestioned presuppositions to which all too many traditional supporters of science are blind.

The defenders of scientistic dogma almost never show any understanding of opponents' frameworks and beliefs, thus making their own position weak and suspect. A classic case is the gross distortion and misunderstanding by the Vienna Circle and similar logicist believers of the point of Wittgenstein's logical analyses in his *Tractatus*. They thought that they had a distinguished, strong ally, but instead they had a brilliant opponent. All that the defenders of the status quo seem to be able to see is the unconventionality of the critics, their violation of scientific truths, beliefs and values that the mainstream takes as obvious, commonsensical, beyond questioning and criticism.[10] To repeat Taylor's point, Condillac

> wouldn't have known where Herder was 'coming from,' just as his heirs today, the proponents of chimp language, talking computers, and truth-conditional theories of meaning, find the analogous objections to their views gratuitous and puzzling.[11]

The ignorance is not symmetrical. It seems obvious that Herder understood where Condillac was coming from. I see the discussions about the neonate as the little scientist as analogous.

It seems that nothing can change scientism. The lines have been drawn, the opponents preach to the choir. It seems obvious to me, though, that in the context of this book, a blind faith in science's potential to rescue the globe and humankind is likely to be not only misplaced but dangerous. Science, non-neutral science, all too often is one of the primary vehicles for mad abstracting, dichotomizing, depersonalizing and reifying. It has played a major role in what has brought us to our present untenable situation.[12] It seems beyond dispute that science and technology's many benefits that are often offered as evidence of their neutrality just aren't nearly enough justification. The benefits fall far short of outweighing the horrors of the Hiroshimas and Nagasakis. I just don't see advances such as those in medicine, dentistry, labor-saving devices, social media gadgetry[13] or air travel as balancing the scales. As Bryan Appleyard says, 'science, more than anything else, has made us who we are; science is our faith and our age's unique signature. My conclusion is equally simple: we must resist and the time to do so is now.'[14] He adds the understatement that 'Less simple is the task of persuading you either of my thesis or my conclusion.' Science's noxious presuppositions and attendant difficulties become one of those things that are too near to be seen. In sum, what the enthusiastic, zealous proponents of science who see it as humanity's savior almost invariably overlook completely, cannot or will not see, are blind to, are the destructive, dominating aspects that unavoidably come with sciencing, the 'putting of nature on the rack'. The torturer disappears; we are left with the illusion of an impersonal, pseudoneutral view from nowhere that cannot be faulted.

The question of science's neutrality that I am advocating is complicated by a contradiction. On the one hand, science does have mostly tacit values, and these have undeniably noxious, destructive consequences. But on the other hand, it *is* neutral, but about values that we need, especially those that have to do with damaging ourselves and our natural world. Some see this obliviousness to human values as beginning with the ejection of the so-called secondary qualities from science's edenic domain, an ejection that arose along with the rise of science itself. Science has nothing to say either about the sanctity of our earth or about the value of life. The bottom line is that we end up with the kind of toxic situation that Heidegger conceptualized in terms of 'standing-reserve': making everything, humanity included, into a dehumanized resource stored for later use (see Chapter 2). The implication is that humanity ought to be very, very careful about relying blindly on scientific-technological solutions. Were we to do so, any amelioration achieved thereby probably may very well be only temporary – a point that I have made before. The madness-making properties of science-technology are carried along in the solution, which would become just one more case of a symptom removal oriented therapy failing because it had been blind to the actual dynamics that generated and maintained the catastrophic threats in the first place. This is not a new argument,[15] but it runs into formidable defensive resistances and so is almost always dismissed for this or that reason. 'Everybody knows it is nonsensical.'

I submit that effective reform cannot be just some symptom-relieving strategy, no matter how credible and commonsensical it might appear. Reforms ought to evolve organically, though not necessarily slowly. They need to rest on a sound contact with reality. As the philosopher Jiddu Krishnamurti put it,

> Reform, however necessary, only breeds the need for further reform, and there is no end to it. What is essential is a revolution in man's thinking, not patchwork reform...If it may be asked, how do you know what's good for the people? You assume so much. You start with so many conclusions; and when you start with a conclusion, whether your own or that of another, all thinking ceases...Every party knows, or thinks it knows, what's good for the people.[16]

If, as I maintain, reforms must rest on a clear view of the realities, then somehow we must jettison the madness whose dominant characteristic (and, probably, also its dominant motivation) is exactly to obscure, distort that clarity. My notion is that what we need to achieve is the sort of sanity that I sketched in Chapter 7. Unfortunately, until then we will not be able to see what it is that we need to do.

Two pathological populations

We have seen that humanity's madness grows out of a complex inter-mingling of two sources: the infant's originary, primal bifurcation, and the grown-ups' distortions that have arisen with humanity's entry into literacy. While this intertwining of origins cannot be ignored, still, the reality is that currently we have two kinds of carriers of our mad-ness – adults and children – and that calls for two different ways of thinking about interventions. We need to think about what can be done to counter the madness of the current, already existing popu-lation of adults. That was the question that I addressed in *Averting Global Extinction*.[17] That work sought to adapt the general psycho-dynamically oriented approach to individual therapy usually called the analysis of defense, to groups and populations. I still think that in principle the approach is sound, but it needs considerable further development and faces great, possibly insurmountable, practical and theoretical difficulties.

I won't attempt to describe that earlier work but will give one example of its implications. Let us return to the matter of the apparently destruc-tive 'selfishness' of those who make our situation worse for their own gratification and profit, the situation that I touched on in Chapter 1. What is the usual remedial approach? Almost invariably it is to try to alter the evildoers' behaviors and ideas, to reform them by one or more of the all-too-familiar standard methods for changing someone's mind and behaviors: force, deceit, cajoling, intimidation and threats, bribery, exile, counterarguments, appealing to their better nature, conferences, negotiations, compromises, treaties and so on. History is pretty clear about the long-term effectiveness of this family of remedies. Destructive selfishness persists.

An alternative that is suggested in part by the analogous situation in individual therapy is the following. As I discussed in Chapter 1, in the context of world-destroying actions, in most cases the 'villains' who commit these selfish acts are not being selfish at all – although they and everyone else might think they are. Realistically, they are being self-destructive. But since, on the surface, these kinds of behavior do seem selfish and noxious to most of us, our usual response is to try to get these selfish entities to change their selfish behavior, give up their self-centeredness and drive for gratification. The results are almost never good. Who would willingly give up greatly satisfying behaviors, especially if one were powerful?

The less obvious, reality-attuned therapeutic approach is to do what we can to make these entities (individuals, corporations, nations) recognize the realities and consequences of their acts, beliefs, policies. If that can be accomplished, if the realization of self-destructiveness were to be deep and not just cognitive, the chances are that we wouldn't have to try to change anything. The others would become motivated to act in accordance with their actual, realistic best interests. We need to begin thinking about how to do that, but that would be a major change in tactic and conception. Entities may and should become truly selfish. That is what we should strive for. All would benefit. We somehow must try to get the point across that what the destructive entities are doing is not in their interests at all, that actually, in reality, it is self-destructive, suicidal, fatal to all. We need to try to understand what produces and maintains these strange delusions. We should insist, hammer away at the point, that their (or is it our?) self-destructive behaviors are unacceptable. We must also step back and re-examine our own part in stimulating the opponent's behavior – a difficult and aversive task. We may have to look at some unpleasant aspects (Al Gore's inconvenient truths) of our own policies, values and behaviors, ones that we tell ourselves are beyond criticism – our rabid nationalism, for instance.

If all parties involved would make survival their top priority issue, if all were to insist that they are simply unwilling to accept mad solutions, then deprived of the usual range of familiar solutions they would be forced to seek and creatively invent previously unthought-of approaches, approaches that heretofore had been masked by our conviction that we were aware of all the possible options. (No new approaches are necessary or possible; we have looked.) If we were to militantly insist that while we don't yet know what to do, but still, that selecting options that virtually guarantee humanity's self-destruction is simply unacceptable, that something other must be found and done, perhaps that would unearth sane, as yet unthought of approaches. It may seem odd, but I am convinced that part of our problem is that we are sure that we know all the realistic, possible options; we are convinced that we have considered everything.

If the participants involved in acting in a self-destructive way really come to understand that their actions will destroy/defeat not only the perceived enemy but also themselves, that the acts are self-destructive, or, alternatively, if they blindly refuse to see the suicidal aspects of their acts, if in either case they still persist on their set course, then we have a real, possibly insurmountable and very likely fatal problem. We have the daunting clinical and practical problem of the deeply suicidal and mad patient (or patients – we might have to include ourselves) writ large. But at least we will have reframed the problem for ourselves. We will no longer try to change the other in presumably commonsensical ways, using the tried and untrue approaches that 'everybody knows are the only realistic ones'. We would not focus on changing behaviors. Because we are dealing with pathology we would be fools not to start thinking clinically. So, in any case, we do need to begin thinking about that madness in ourselves and others, and to think about its 'therapy'. (I am well aware of the limitations of self-therapy, but here we don't have much choice.)

How to start? To begin with, how might we approach our own madness? After all, presumably it is more accessible than the madness of others. I raised this question in the concluding remarks of a recent paper on psychiatry's severely flawed conceptual foundations. After outlining what I saw as its core problems, I asked:

> So where do we go from here? When Heidegger lectured about almost anything – language, things, technology, and of course especially Being, he invariably insisted that our ideas about it are correct but not true, that we hadn't even begun to think. Consequently, he famously recommended to first dwell with the subject of one's concern, to allow it to speak to us, to follow its lead. In a similar quietist vein, Alan Watts told us that the question 'What shall we do about it?' is only asked by those who do not understand the problem. He said that if a problem can be solved at all, to understand it and to know what to do about it are the same thing.[18] Robert Oppenheimer is said to have remarked shortly before his death that the only thing that may prevent our world from going to hell where it is obviously headed, is to do absolutely nothing to try to stop that descent. He was no fool. To those who might be interested in expanding on this strange armature I have begun to articulate and explore [my recommendations to psychiatrists], I would invert the old exhortation and say: Don't just do something – stand there! – at least for openers.[19]

In sum, we should start with the Hippocratic Oath's *primum non nocere* – first, do no harm. Perhaps the first thing that each of us needs to do initially is to stop, take a break, step back from driven activity and get acquainted with our madness. I believe that what I am suggesting is very much in the spirit of Heidegger's conception of 'dwelling with'. It is a non-cognitive, pretheoretical, prethematizing, receptive immersion in, and becoming attuned to, one's madness, letting it come more compellingly into view, letting it open up its own path: 'The point is not to listen to a series of propositions, but rather to follow the movement of showing.'[20] This sounds unacceptably passive, mystical, vague, unhelpful, anti-American (doing nothing is unacceptable in our fanatically 'just-do-it-ist' culture).[21] I see the process of defusing madness as beginning by increasingly becoming alert and sensitive to the presence and impact of our own chronic distorting, abstracting and reifying, by becoming acutely aware of the illusions created by the received view of language – particularly by its separatist and referential assumptions. We need to try to recognize it as mad when we see and use language as a separable, autonomous, referential tool, and thereby depersonalize, fragment, estrange, distort, reify – create mythical entities to investigate, define, worry and fight about. We need to stop treating language as magical. Think of all of the situations where an acoustic signal or scribble is taken as a major real entity, either as positive (the 'I do' of witnesses in court) or negative (pejorative language of all kinds – declarations of war, for example).

Dwelling with would also include trying to see the incoherently split ways in which we typically see ourselves (the observer observing inner and outer events). We may catch a glimpse, have an experiential moment of a state in which 'it is no longer clear what we might mean by either "language" or "being" '.[22] That could be progress, although vertiginous at first. The premise is that trying to gain some empathy with our objectifying, abstracting madness in these or any other appropriate ways might launch us on a journey toward more realistic, integrated, non-dual perceptions of self, world and language. Then perhaps we could also see what we realistically and productively could and should do to help to defuse the threats that we face.

Childhood and parenting

'Einstein was once asked, "What can we do to get a better world?" He replied, "You have to have better people." '[23] I see this as a profound, simple, even obvious truth and insight, one that we ought to ponder. I submit that the Pirahã offer a model for such a community of 'better people'. One way to fix the world's problems, then, would simply be for all of us to imitate these superbly functioning people. That is out of the question, for any number of reasons. First of all, it can't be done.

Second, it would be a case of symptom removal. Perhaps the next best thing, then, and something that may be more doable, is to consider how the Pirahã get to be the kinds of people they are and see what that can teach us. In other words, it might be instructive to look at Pirahã parenting and childhood.

Everett is not a clinician and his observations of Pirahã children and parenting are quite superficial, but he does give homely examples that are suggestive if one is able to read between the lines. A close, psychodynamically informed reading of some of his descriptions can offer clues about how it is that the children turn into such admirable, sane adults.

I should point out from the start, though, that the facts and implications of these examples of parenting probably will not sit well with most adults in our mad culture. The Pirahã approaches, views, values and mores go against many of our sacred cows, our sentimental and zealously held views about children, childhood in general, and parenting. One of the signal but unrecognized symptoms of our madness is our unrealistic view of children and childhood that infects our parenting and teaching. This is a very big topic, and I can only touch on it here. How do we consider children and childhood? First, as we began to see in Chapter 3, we abet the child's early bifurcation, its splitting into two strangely related selves: the elusive, infinitely regressing observer self that cannot see itself, and that also is the observable stage on which all kinds of events can and do presumably happen. It is the 'little Douglas over there, in the mirror', the locus of actions, where events and processes can and do take place, where the spurious, grossly misleading 'states' (pains, wishes, thoughts) that Wittgenstein warned us about come into being. It is the same stage as the one on which supposedly quite different kinds of event also take place: representations, events arising from things that presumably are happening outside ourselves (both selves?) – the things we call 'our perceptions of the outside world', the origins in our standard causal theories of perception. It is the stage on which little Douglas observes his other. The stage is the locus of thoughts, concepts, ideas, pains, qualia and sense data. The observer of all this is who? This is the incoherent mess, significantly aggravated still further by the received view of language and its simplistically seen referential capability. I see this confused underlying incoherence as responsible for the unending contentious and pretentious philosophical realist/antirealist debates that were referred to earlier, as well as for the many other debates that are offshoots of this morass.[24]

The implanting of this incoherent view is one way of looking at the origin of the madness. There is also another, related aspect of the mad parenting process – namely, a severely distorted conception of child-hood. Broad sectors of our civilization have come to regard and treat children as some sort of exotic breed, almost non-human, Martian, only distantly related to adults: a child, not really a person. Parents and adults, as well as the children themselves, buy into this false and noxious dichotomy. We become unrealistically sentimental about child-hood (while at the same time condoning widespread violence and illness that so many of the world's children are enduring). We all tacitly agree, mostly without careful examination, that childhood is special. Children require all sorts of special considerations, protection, sheltering from realities and stress (from witnessing sexual activity, for example). We talk to them in special, infantilizing ways – 'baby talk'. I am of course not suggesting that there are no differences between children and adults, that we ought to let toddlers play in traffic, but I *am* saying that the differences that we identify and attend to are to a great extent unrealis-tic, grossly distorted and damaging to all concerned. These conceptions of child-raising and its implementation are very important matters, another notable but difficult-to-spot constellation of symptoms of our wholesale distortion of reality.

In this view of childhood and the associated approaches to parent-ing, in most families from the moment a child is born or perhaps even sooner, that human being tends to be treated as unique, different, spe-cial, requiring and justifying preferential treatment in all sorts of ways, fussed over, but also needing almost constant control and supervision. At least for the first decade of its life the child is dealt with in innumer-able ways as something basically quite unlike an adult – as a special almost non-human, non-person species of a sort: it is a 'child' first, almost a property. The reality that first of all a child is a human being (which few would deny, but also few really believe in practice), albeit with significant limitations and immaturities, is a fact that gets lost in the shuffle. Few adults see children, let alone their own child, as sim-ply just a person first. In our culture, the child is almost sure to be fed narcissism-supporting fables. For example, it is told that when it grows up it can be whatever it wants to be, if it only wants it badly enough. (Even the notion that in order to achieve its ambitions the child will have to work also tends to get lost in the shuffle. Wishing ought to be enough. The child is special, unique, has magic [computer-enhanced] powers. Entitlement and narcissism take over.)[25] It learns all sorts of myths and acquires all sorts of nefarious abstractions. Many children become chauvinists early on – about family and outsiders, country, reli-gion, social class, school, professions, sports teams. The child learns our insane values concerning money, possessions, success. All of this special, unrealistic treatment of childhood has significant, and I strongly believe by and large highly undesirable, consequences.

One of these is that, given how it is treated, the child quite naturally assumes not only that it is fundamentally radically different from adults but that something special has to happen, or it has to do something spectacular, to change its status, to become that magical other, the adult. Thus the created split often remains unhealed in the adult, causing no end of mischief, visible and invisible. This remaining chasm between idealized childhood and adult personhood plays into the evolution of our madness in innumerable, complex not always easy-to-recognize ways. (As far as I know, it has remained an unrecognized and major problem in psychiatric and other therapeutic thought – at least I have never seen it described or discussed in the literature.)

Here is where we can begin to use the Pirahã parenting as an example. Before contrasting their parenting with ours, however, I do want to explicitly caution that even if their ways were vastly preferable to ours, they would not be palatable to most of us – at least not on first encounter. That should come as no surprise. Our parenting ways, like just about everything else we do, are mad. If Pirahã parenting is sane, then it will almost automatically be threatening to us. It will need to be fended off, attacked, and our ways will need to be aggressively defended.

Basically, although allowances are made for their size and relative physical weakness, by and large Pirahã children, even very young ones, are not considered to be qualitatively different from adults. This is evident right from the child's birth. Children are first of all considered to be human beings, just like everyone else. They have no special status. They are treated fairly and realistically. Baby talk doesn't exist. Infants as well as older children are spoken to in the same tone and treated with the same respect that we in our Western society use between adults (when we aren't killing or screaming at each other). A kind of laissez-faire position is taken toward the child from the beginning. With a toddler, a mother may just sit and watch her baby walk straight for a fire. A low-key warning, a guttural note of disapproval, may be nonchalantly issued, but that's as far as the mother's parenting and protecting goes. She stops there, letting the baby get scorched if it fails to behave realistically. (Usually it remains unharmed, behaves appropriately – realistically.) Similarly, adults do not prevent a two-year-old child from playing with a sharp kitchen knife. In one case reported by Everett, when a boy was playing with such a knife and dropped it, the mother even picked it up and handed it back to him. In these kinds of situation – situations that we almost certainly would not allow to develop in the first place – children rarely hurt themselves seriously, but the kids do cut themselves, get help, learn. Another example is that although adults rarely smoke or drink, on rare occasions Everett saw such strange sights as a three-year-old smoking a cigarette hand-rolled by his father, or little kids getting drunk along with everyone else.

The overriding principle that governs the Pirahã's entirely unsentimental and aggressively realistic parenting policies is acting in ways that develop independence, toughness, attuned responses to their great teacher, nature, environmental reality. They let death weed out weaklings, let the kids learn to take care of themselves. In this environment you have to get tough or die. (For us, this of course is unacceptable, inhuman. So much for letting reality be the guide.) Children are equal citizens and have to obey the same rules as adults, but that works both ways. The policy is to let nature and the natural consequences of their actions be the child's main teachers, much along the lines recommended by Alfred Adler, the Austrian physician and therapist who developed the school of individual psychology that had distinguished followers such as Albert Ellis, Victor Frankl and Rollo May.[26] Everyone in the Pirahã culture learns to pull their own weight, almost from infancy. These are tough lessons and tough policies, but children are considered equals to adults no later than when they're weaned in the Pirahã tribe. And they grow into healthy adults, non-philosophers, apparently (so far) escaping both the ontogenetic and the phylogenetic roots of our madness. As I said, according to Everett they are superbly, happily, productive, competently functioning people attuned to, and doing very well in, a difficult, challenging, ever dangerous environment.

Child weaning is a traumatic experience for the kids; it is a tough rite of passage. Crying and pleading for milk is ignored, forcing the child early to learn to find its own food. Toughness is necessary for jungle life, and learning quickly is imperative to the Pirahã's survival. Children are free to roam, are considered to be everyone's responsibility, are treated with affection and respect. They are rarely disciplined. They are not considered to be special or precious. Neither are they seen as the unique property of their parents. That does not mean that they are free to do as they please, however. As I said, the same prohibitions apply to them as to adults, and vice versa. Children are given freedom of choice, but usually they eventually learn that it is useful to listen to adults. There is an

Undercurrent of Darwinism [that] produces very tough and resilient adults who do not believe that anyone owes them anything...[there is] no coddling, ameliorating [of] hurts...if a kid gets hurt, it is scolded and cared for too ... Children are just human beings in Pirahã society, as worthy of respect as any fully grown human adult. They are not seen as in need of coddling or special protections.[27] *Israel Bettelheim*

An important concomitant of this view of childhood and these approaches to rearing children (or rather, allowing them to mature naturally) is that the kind of estranging, distancing mad dualism that accompanies literacy is not evident in these children as infants, nor does it develop as they mature. As I have said, that does not mean that Pirahã adults and children aren't appropriately aware of their world – far from it. It does mean, however, that they don't engage gratuitously in bifurcating, in reflexive thinking, in mental gymnastics, in pathology-generating self-reflection. Aristotle's general statement to the effect that the human being is a being that wants to know, to seek answers to philosophical questions, may well be a symptomatic manifestation of Western madness and not characteristic of the species. From Everett's many descriptions and comments, I would guess that in terms of the model proposed in Chapter 7, most of the time the Pirahã are in the mode of sanity that borders on non-duality. They eschew gratuitous abstracting and cognizing. I would also guess that, as needed, the Pirahã are quite capable of reflecting, stepping back, disengaging and temporarily shifting to the second mode of sanity, the mode that at least superficially resembles our mad, rigid science-like position. In sum, my guess is that the Pirahã's way of being in the world is much like the hypothetical model of sanity sketched earlier: a fluid back-and-forth movement between a non-thematizing, integrated, a-analytical non-duality on the one hand and a state that is closer to our familiar formalizing, abstracting and structuring on the other, as needed. The movement is governed by the demands of reality – of the 'really real'. Their example is stimulating and suggestive, but it also brings us face to face with sanity's inscrutability.

How might we translate these observations into parenting approaches that would be desirable, accepted and doable in our mad culture? We are stuck with literacy; there is no possibility of aping p-orality, regressing. I will not attempt to map out a strategy for how our parenting might be changed into parenting that in its essentials was modeled on the Pirahã's ways. Such an exploration is beyond the scope of this book, but seems well worth undertaking. In any case, the example of the Pirahã strongly suggests that the 'little Douglas' split into madness's foundation is not inevitable, not somehow innate to humans. If it were, we would find the same kind of madness in the Pirahã that we find in our culture, and it seems clear that we don't. Everett unwittingly provides many examples supporting this conclusion, such as the tribe's adamant, militant, successful refusal to become literate, or to pay attention to anything that seems gratuitously speculative, or irrelevant. So, as I see it, the big problem with transmuting Pirahã parenting into a version tailored to us literates is not that such a reconstruction would be all that difficult. What is more than likely to be very difficult is to convince a mad culture to even consider making a drastic change in parenting. (We know it all, and, what we don't know, science can tell us.) Nevertheless, I would expect that task, as difficult as it would likely be, still to be easier than changing other aspects of adults' madness. It may be easier to convince the world's adult population to give up some of its destructive parenting dogmas and practices than to stop it from polluting the earth, or waging incredibly (self-)destructive wars.[28]

The most promising approach to ameliorating our looming dangers, then, is to grow a sane world population via substantially changed approaches to child-raising. The obstacles are severe and daunting. For one thing, it would take time – both to bring about the change in parenting and to have a new generation of children become adult, and we may not have very much time left. For another, the attempt will run into a reflexive paradox: Sane parenting takes sane parents. At present we have few, if any. If these were already plentiful, we wouldn't be facing global extinction. I also mentioned that, things being what they are, it is to be expected, almost guaranteed, that in general any attempt to challenge and significantly change a mad population's mad ways, parenting included, would arouse severe resistance.[29] I repeat Steven Bartlett's comments cited in Chapter 1:

> Central to human pathology is human resistance to an awareness of it. 'Denial' would be an understatement, for the forces that stand in the way of humankind's reflective consciousness of the psychological and ecological malignancy of the species are incredibly strong, tenacious, and self-preserving.

> As a result of human recalcitrance to acknowledge our own pathology, in the history of behavioral science, and in particular in the history of psychology and psychiatry, almost no effort has been made to gain an understanding of human pathology that has its roots in *normal* – as opposed to abnormal – *psychology*.[30]

The fundamental conundrum is that in order to be able to provide something like Pirahã parenting, the mad adult population would first have had to change, at least in some important respects. Our adults' parenting would need to become much more realistic, much less inconsistently both oversentimental and simultaneously unacceptably callous (think of our indifference to the world's multitude of sick and starving children, or the many instances of severe abuse).

Even if parenting practices were to change for the better, bringing about significant therapeutic changes in an entire population by growing different kinds of person would require considerable time at best, as I have already noted. But an experience that I had about 50 years ago is food for thought. I referred to it in a recent publication:

> I began in the early 1960s to occasionally make small attempts over the years to interest any planners who were addressing global dangers, especially the nuclear threat, in expanding their standard approaches by injecting psychodynamic thinking into their approaches. My first attempts, made long before I began formal studies in psychology, were made in 1962 during several Boston meetings of the nuclear physicist Leo Szilard's 'Council for Abolishing War,' later renamed the 'Council for a Livable World.' At those meetings, my suggestions that psychological factors ought to be incorporated into the approaches the organization was developing and recommending, were disdainfully dismissed out of hand: It is naive to think that psychological factors and measures could be consequential in the Council's endeavors; psychologists and psychotherapists need to remain in their bailiwick – which, incidentally, is a view still shared by many of my colleagues...a second kind of objection voiced in the Council meetings was that incorporating psychological considerations or approaches would be much too slow. The problems were too pressing; time was too short; immediately effective measures were called for. Well, here we are, almost 50 years later [now more than 50 years], and we are no better off; we are still in mortal danger, still relying on the strategy of mutually assured destruction (M.A.D.), surely as psychotic a policy as its acronym implies. We remain at the stage where the best advice we can offer to school children still is that were a nuclear attack imminent, they should duck under their desks. So much for lacking the time to explore unconventional approaches...[31]

To conclude these considerations about parenting, I want to comment on fear. Pirahã parenting shows us that we overprotect our children from reality, and that the consequences are not desirable. There are of course some limits to the realities that a child can or should be expected to tolerate, but just what these are often isn't easy to establish in specific instances. I am sure, though, that in that regard our parenting is madly bifurcated, just like in everything else. On the one hand, we err considerably on the side of detrimental, reality-distorting and -obscuring maudlin coddling. It shouldn't be hard to see how that abets madness – grandiosity, for example. On the other hand, we mistreat and damage our children in innumerable ways, beginning with the introduction into a life of passive perception, mad materialism, easy omnipotent control, self-estrangement, hyperactivity, hyperrationality, and muddying of reality by the use of electronic gadgetry and media.

I want to focus on the coddling pole of this dyad. The practice of trying to protect our children from fear seems beyond criticism, but in reality it is a rigid, ill-conceived, black-and-white, all-or-none, poor and dangerous policy. It is one thing to be appropriately protective, but quite another to abet fundamental distortions of reality, denying dangers that must be faced and thus leading to a highly inappropriate comfort, sense of safety. One of the major consequences of this unrealistic protectionism is that an approach originally intended to apply to children has drifted and has come to be applied universally. Now we downplay for everybody the fearful realities of nuclear wars, of ecological disasters (oil spills, disintegrating nuclear plants), of growing poisoned food. Believers in UFOs claim that one reason why governments suppress evidence of their existence is that they are afraid that the information would cause widespread panic reminiscent of Orson Wells' 'The War of the Worlds' radio broadcast. All such 'considerate' protective measures contribute to the fatal weakening of our perception of reality – and remove the motivation to engage in preventive measures. Nothing frightens us any longer (or it frightens us so badly that we must deny reality). There is no end to the reassurances that just about all dangers can be averted – typically by means of science and technology, but also often by one or another sort of magic. At any rate, there are no dangers; all this talk about dangers is nefarious propaganda or crazy doomsday talk. We continue to rely on measures that are analogous to those preposterous ones that were recommended to schoolchildren at the height of the Cold War. They were instructed to duck under their desks in case of a nuclear attack. Educational documentaries illustrating these measures were produced. Drills were performed. I believe that the underlying policies and assumptions remain unchanged, although the recommendations may have been modified. (On second thoughts, now there are none.) Now

I ask you, how much more evidence do we need of just how mad we have become?

I do have some guarded how-to suggestions in this context. First, we need to stop mechanically repeating to ourselves that 'we have nothing to fear but fear itself', comforting ourselves with that mantra. This much quoted reassurance, supposedly given by Franklin Delano Roosevelt during the Depression, is actually truncated and misleading. What Roosevelt did say was much more realistic:

> So, first of all, let me assert my firm belief that the only thing we have to fear is fear itself – nameless, unreasoning, unjustified terror which paralyzes needed efforts to convert retreat into advance.[32]

'Unjustified terror', but in our age, terror is far from unjustified. The suppression of justified, appropriate fear is enormously damaging. It removes needed motivation to address pressing issues and abets reality distortion. One ordinary, simple, unpleasant lesson implied by the analyses of madness is that we should be very frightened indeed by our current circumstances and not turn away from them. If humanity's response to such exposure were to be paralysis, then the likely consequences are not difficult to see. They are essentially the same ones that follow from pretending that there is no reason to be afraid and then doing nothing for *that* reason. The turning away from fear is very much like the self-destructive behavior masquerading as selfishness. Both are blind to impending catastrophe; indeed they abet it.

The world of paradox

I believe that the most noteworthy feature of the material presented in this and previous chapters is the perpetual reappearance of paradox and its close cousin ineffability. In the framework that I have laid out, the root sources were the two developmental events gone awry that fracture and fragment a previously existing ineffable integration: the child's ontogenetic move into the language dimension, and humankind's phylogenetic move into the world of literacy. Each in its own way emerges from an unimaginable prior reality and gives birth to a paradoxically reflexive/reflective nefarious core that can be neither clarified nor removed by cognition, logic, science, philosophy. We now live irreversibly in a world of artificial and madness-inducing pseudo-realities, pseudoproblems, splits, dichotomies, depersonalization, alienations, dehumanizations. We struggle with paradoxical self-reference, with sentences such as 'All Cretans are liars', 'This sentence is false', Gödel sentences – all grounded in the suspect separability assumption. Once it has come into existence, that bifurcated and bifurcating core proliferates silently, growing out of sight at an exponential rate, silently launching us on a disastrous path. The resulting wholesale failure of reality-testing, the pathology of normality, puts us on the road to disaster.

These fracturing features of madness appeared over and over in the previous discussions. The emphasis has been on the consequences that this madness has for global survival, but in fact the nefarious impacts of this madness are destructively at work in just about every situation, in all professions and disciplines, in most ordinary, everyday dealings. Therefore I believe its presence, nature and origins ought to be a central concern in virtually all disciplines and professions. (Their local concerns could join up with the global versions.) Identifying and understanding the mad perspective can help to identify and illuminate paradoxes in the natural sciences (quantum theory's observer problems, for example), certainly in the fields that purport to deal with human beings,[33] and, surprisingly, even in fields such as mathematics and logic that at first glance seem autonomous, devoid of human influence, a view strongly shared by most of the fields' experts. (Most mathematicians see themselves as discoverers of the really real, not the makers of reality: their subject matter is autonomous, found and not made, utterly divorced from subjectivity – mathematics' *bête noir* is psychologism, after all.)[34] In short, I see the approaches developed here in the large context of global dangers as very widely relevant and applicable in numerous narrower contexts as well.

Our ubiquitous forgetting of the presence of persons in all situations pervades our world. We forget, or don't want to recognize in the first place, that as William James put it, 'The trail of the human serpent is thus over everything.'[34] Perhaps something like that is what Heidegger had in mind with his constant talk about the 'forgetting of Being', or with his concept of enframing, technological thinking. In his 1966 interview with *Der Spiegel*, he famously said that only a god can save us. The complete quote is even more bleak:

> Philosophy will not be able to bring about a direct change of the present state of the world. This is true not only of philosophy but of all merely human meditations and endeavors. Only a god can still save us. I think the only possibility of salvation left to us is to prepare readiness, through thinking and poetry, for the appearance of the

god or for the absence of the god during the decline; so that we do not, simply put, die meaningless deaths, but that when we decline, we decline in the face of the absent god.

Could the mere addition of the clinical-developmental dimension to mainstream thinking and its underlying frameworks make the needed difference, stall or even reverse the trend? Can this corrective to our perspectives serve as a surrogate for the still absent deity? That is a large, very likely grandiose, presumption indeed. The odds that this widening of perspective will make such a drastic difference are not good – but then, one never knows for sure. One can hope. Let us dwell, and see.

Notes

1 Understanding Our Global Dangers

1. Chomsky and Polk (2013, p. 13).
2. Aitkenhead (2008).
3. The Fukushima nuclear plant and the Gulf oil spill disasters are obvious and adequate examples.
4. See, for example, Bartlett (2011), Kohn (June 1988), Baumeister and Bushman (2004).
5. It may seem indefensible to question science/technology's efficacy. However, the belief that science can deal with all problems and has all the answers is scientistic dogma – see Hughes (2012); Thompson (1981). Extended arguments against it will be presented later. The key point is that science is grounded in any number of presuppositions that are axiomatic, taken for granted as self-evident, as incontrovertible, or have remained unnoticed and unexamined. It, like any belief system, rests on an unprovable axiomatic basis.
6. Einstein (1960, p. 185).
7. Ibid. For critiques of scientism in psychology and psychoanalysis, see Berger (1985a; 2002a,b).
8. Einstein, p. 185.
9. Ibid., p. 189.
10. According to Freud, both kinds of instinct are immutable – but, surprisingly, also indispensable.
11. His proposal was to take actions that would 'stimulate the erotic instincts' – in popular terms, to encourage loving feelings, solidarity, benign group identifications and feelings of community – Einstein, pp. 185–203.
12. We will see that this traditional view has been seriously challenged by more recent thought and evidence.
13. Einstein, p. 201.
14. Hinshaw (1949, pp. 652, 655).
15. Segal (1995, p. 7).
16. Schumacher (1977, p. 42).
17. Picchi (2013) and Engdahl (2007).
18. Berger (1991, 1985a).
19. Freud (1961/1930, pp. 141–142) and Bartlett (2011, pp. 16–18).
20. Berger (2009, 1991, 1985b, 1970). See also Freud (1961/1930), Fromm (1955), Lasch (1979), Kovel (2007). For a work that foreshadows the development-based analyses to be presented here, see Shepard (1982) and Berger (2009).
21. Lasch.
22. American Psychiatric Association (2013); PDM Task Force (2006).
23. Wittgenstein (1969–1975, p. 141).

24. Bartlett (2011, p. 9). For an excellent analysis, see the section entitled 'Psychological resistance to the abandonment of psychological normality as mental health' (2011, pp. 241–244). See also Berger (2009) on the general topic of defensive resistance.
25. Cahoone (1988, pp. 8–9).
26. Olafson (1995, p. 16).
27. Ellis (1993, pp. 45, 15).
28. Thomson (2005, p. 56).
29. Quoted in Braver (2012, p. 24).
30. Guignon (1983, P. 30).
31. Berger (2011a and 2012).
32. Berger (2011a, Chapter 7).
33. Lawson (1985, p. 9).
34. Wittgenstein (1969–1975, p. 56). For illuminating discussions and interpretations of Wittgenstein's use of "nonsense" see Mulhall (2007).

2   What Is Language and Why Does It Matter?

1. Harris (1990, p. 180). His snide reference to 'defectives' seems ill-advised.
2. Wittgenstein (1958, §93).
3. Monk (2005, p. 37).
4. McGinn (2009, p. 162).
5. Wittgenstein (1969–1975, no. 467).
6. Candlish and Wrisley (2012); Mulhall (2007).
7. Guignon (1983, p. 32).
8. Lafont (2000, p. xi).
9. Ian Robinson calls it 'linguistic atomism' (1975, p. 2).
10. Ellis (1993, p. 9); also Berger (2011a, Chapter 2; 1985a, Chapter 4).
11. Guignon (1983, p. 32). Writing from a similar perspective, the philosopher Frederick Olafson calls this conception of language the 'logicolinguistic point of view' (1995, p. 3).
12. Berger (2011a).
13. Harris (1996) calls this problematic reflexivity 'metalinguistic' usage, and raises serious questions about the legitimacy of using it in linguistic theorizing.
14. Roughly, these properties reflect the realist view that Braver specifies by means of his realism matrix – Braver (2007, p. xix).
15. A prime example is Ian Robinson's detailed, telling critique of Chomskian theorizing. He starts by questioning the claim that linguistics is based 'on a complete collection of facts', posing the question rarely asked in linguistics, or for that matter anywhere else: how 'one knows a fact when one sees one' (1975, p. 2).
16. Berger (2011a, especially chapters 6 and 7).
17. Everett (2008).
18. A notable example is his discussion of 'dual patterning'. This clearly shows his atomistic, structural-grammatical-logical conception of language – Everett, p. 198.

19. Everett, pp. 17, 201.
20. Olafson (1995, pp. 47, 49, 125).
21. Kusch (1995); Berger (2011a, pp. 72–77).
22. Ellis (1993, pp. 95–96); Berger (2011a, pp. 114–126).
23. The quote is from Harris (1996, p. 12). The separability assumption is a key topic and target of criticism in Berger (2011a).
24. Olafson (1995, p. 8).
25. Nagel (1986).
26. Guignon, p. 24.
27. For a refreshing antidote to what he calls 'neurophilosophy', see Tallis (1999 a, b; 2008).
28. Guignon, p. 19.
29. Harris (1996, pp. 12, 29, 33).
30. Taylor (1995, p. 102).
31. Harris (2005, p. 3).
32. Lawson (2001, p. 59).
33. Guignon (1983).
34. For an excellent brief overview, see Sadler (2005, pp. 234–236).
35. Thomson (2005, p. 7).
36. Ibid., p. 59.
37. Stanislav Grof's thinking is a compelling example – see Grof (2000; 1985).
38. Barrett (1978); Thomson (2009 and 2005); Heidegger (1993); Lovitt and Lovitt (1995); Dreyfus (1997); Young(2002, chapter 3); Braver (2007, pp. 306–314, 317–325).
39. Guignon, p. 189.
40. Dreyfus (1997, p. 99).
41. Kovel (2007).
42. My first exploration was Berger (1974). Subsequent elaborations are in Berger (1978; 1995a and b; 1985a, pp. 40–44).
43. Laplace (1902, p. 4). Until the development of quantum theory it had been used exclusively as a deterministic model, but it serves equally well as a probabilistic model.
44. I discussed the limitations of this model in more recent publications as well – Berger (2002a, especially chapters 1, 3, 5, 22; also 1995). For a comprehensive overview of state process formalisms in science and their role in attempts to explain consciousness, see Thompson (1981, especially chapter 3).
45. My dissertation, prepared when I returned to graduate school mid-life, showed that, and how, this state process formalism model was the underlying structure in the major observational systems that at the time were used in psychotherapy research – Berger (1974). The person is the point, their psychological state at any given moment is that momentary state's coordinate values, and therapy is conceptualized as providing the laws that govern the point's motion through state space. That this model underlies mainstream conceptions of therapy was obvious to me because of my extensive training and experience in natural science, engineering and mathematics. My criticisms came later – Berger (1978; 2002b; 1995a,b).

46. Braver (2007).
47. Wittgenstein (1958, §308).

3   Infancy and First Language Acquisition

1. Ingram (1989, p. 1).
2. Ingram, Chapter 5; Ginsburg and Opper (1988).
3. As we will see, ultimately Wittgenstein dealt with the problem of first language learning by leaving the scene, and advising his peers to do likewise. He said that considerations of that kind of history do not belong in philosophy.
4. Robinson (1975, p. ix).
5. Heidegger (1996).
6. This is a ubiquitous paradox. One form: How did life evolve from inert, lifeless matter?
7. Quoted in Monk (2005, p. 79).
8. This is the assumption I will be calling 'adultocentric'.
9. Again, an adultocentric position.
10. McGinn (2013, pp. 40, 42, 55, 69).
11. Dromm (2006, p. 76)
12. I return to the matter of experiencing in Chapter 4.
13. Taylor (1995, Chapter 5).
14. Taylor (1985a, p. 89).
15. Bouveresse (1995).
16. Berger (2011b).
17. That is not to say that I am one of psychoanalysis' zealous, fanatical true believers – see, for example, Berger (2012, 2002a and b, 2000, 1991, 1985a, 1978). I do believe, though, that most critiques of psychoanalysis are 'uninformed dismissals' – see Braver (2007, p. 4).
18. Romanos (1983, pp. 176–177).
19. Ibid., p. 45.
20. This dichotomizing is an oversimplification. There are genetic theories that still lead to designative theories of language. Piaget is a notable example. Since these kinds of theory retain the received view of language, I will ignore them.
21. Taylor (1985a, pp. 139–140).
22. Because invariably they retain the received view of language, I see the so-called genetic theories such as Piaget's as really incremental theories in disguise. To pursue this issue would take us too far afield and yield little insight.
23. Taylor, p. 140.
24. Berger (2011a, pp. 3–4, 53–61).
25. Nagel (1974).
26. Let us recall Heidegger's caveats about commonsense cited in Chapter 1.
27. Again, the discontinuities of normal science's genetic theories are apparent only.
28. Bolton and Hill (2003, pp. 223–224, 229); see also Quine (1960, Chapter 1); Macnamara (1999, pp. 262–263).
29. Eagleton (2003, p. 61).

30. Guignon (1983, p. 123).
31. Goleman (1992).
32. Chamberlain (1998, p. xiii).
33. Nugent (2013), Nugent and Morell (2011); Carey (2011); Lakoff and Núñez (2000, pp. 15–16,19); Wakeley, Rivera and Langer (2000).
34. Heidegger (1996).
35. That may or may not be logically entailed, but it seems preordained nevertheless.
36. Taylor (1995, Chapter 5; 1985, Chapter 6); see also Guignon, p. 123. The literature that is grounded in and supports incremental/designative views is huge – see, for example, Kuhl (2000), or Ingram (1989).
37. Heidegger (1996).
38. This is precisely the distinction which Guignon made in the citation quoted above.
39. Wittgenstein (1958, §293).
40. Tallis (2012). At best, neuroscience is correlative. That is all it can be. For a broad conceptual analysis supporting this claim see Thompson (1981).
41. Berger (2011a).
42. Guignon (1983, p. 123).
43. Taylor (1985a, pp. 218–219).
44. Collins (2010, pp. 1, x).
45. Taylor (1995, p. 101).
46. Ibid. (1985a, p. 239; 1995, p. 99).
47. Berger (2002a, b; 1995a; 1991; 1985a).
48. Freud (1961/1930, p. 38).
49. Ibid., p. 30.
50. Ibid., pp. 39–41.
51. Loewald, p. 215. I learned a very great deal about therapy from Loewald's writings during my training, and only recently learned that he had studied with Heidegger. Apparently he learned much more from Heidegger than Heidegger did from him, and in my opinion the latter thereby missed a great opportunity. Heidegger's work could have profited greatly by integrating psychodynamic thought about very early development with his own ahistorical notions of being.
52. Fink (1995, p. 6).
53. Bernstein (1992, p. 19).
54. The critical literature is huge – see, for example, Prado (1992); Barrett (1986); Abram (1997); Smith (2001); Olafson (1995); Tallis (1999 a, b).
55. Barrett, 1996.
56. Berger (2011a).
57. Freud, pp. 37, 41, 42.
58. Ibid., p. 37.
59. Loewald (1980, pp. 9, 135).
60. Grof (2000, p. 20).
61. As a clinician, I am against 'how-to' therapeutic recipes and find his later techniques, especially his 'holotropic breath work', uncongenial. But that is only a personal predilection.
62. It may 'unfold' slowly, but still, it *is* a change in kind.
63. Mahler, Pine, and Bergman (1975, p. 3).

64. Wittgenstein (1969–1971, # 141).
65. Rorty (1991, p. 52).
66. Braver (2012). For example, 'If I have exhausted the justifications I have reached bedrock, and my spade is turned. Then I am inclined to say: "This is simply what I do" ' – Wittgenstein (1958, §217).
67. Braver (2007). We will look further at the issue of illusion in Chapter 5, when we begin to discuss the root of the infant's madness in our culture.
68. See Loy (1988) for a comprehensive and approachable account.
69. Taylor (1985a, p. 89).
70. My official major area in graduate school was general-experimental psychology. See also Berger (1981).
71. An analogous, much more complex but essentially quite similar critique can be made of interpretations of observed brain activity in older children and adults that equate neurobiological data and human experiencing – see Tallis (1999a, b, Chapter 2).
72. Taylor (1995, Chapter 5).
73. Bermúdez (2003).
74. From an anonymous book review of Bermúdez (2003) on Amazon.com .
75. Bermúdez, p. 192.
76. Tallis (1999a); Chalmers (1997).
77. Chalmers (1997); Grof (2000); Varela, Thompson and Rosch (1991); McGinn (1999); Thompson (1981).

4   Literacy and Primary Orality

1. Ong (1986, pp. 33–34).
2. Havelock (1986, p. 1).
3. Soukup (2013, p. 39).
4. Ong, p. 24.
5. Harris (2000, pp. 13–14).
6. Ibid., p. 235.
7. Olson (1994, p. 22); see also Olson (2006). I fail to see how he could know that.
8. Scribner and Cole (1981).
9. Ong (1982, pp. 76, 2, 11, 31, 33).
10. See Chapter 2.
11. Havelock, pp. 44, 45.
12. Ong (1982, p. 49).
13. Ibid., Chapter 3.
14. I am borrowing this a- notation from Pauli Pylkkö (1998).
15. Robinson (1975, p. 2).
16. Ibid., p. 4.
17. Ong, p. 77.
18. Ibid., p. 71.
19. Ibid., pp. 24–25.
20. Guignon (1983, pp. 13–14).
21. Baumann (1986, pp. 3–4).
22. Ong, p. 24.

23. Ibid. (1988, p. 260; 1986, p. 24).
24. Ibid., p. 36.
25. Ibid., pp. 37–43; see also Pearl (2013).
26. The idea that language is not made up of words (supposedly one of language's major fundamental building blocks) is an echo of the idea that neonatal experience is unstructured.
27. For radical alternative conceptions, see Noë (2010); Sheldrake (2003).
28. Braver (2007) presents an admirable, comprehensive chronicle and close analysis. It, and similar analyses, will be the starting point for the unconventional comments on reality in Chapter 6, adumbrated in Chapter 1.
29. Tallis (1999a, pp. 82–83).
30. See Olafson (1995, Chapter 1) for a thorough and insightful analysis of the two logically incompatible pictures of the perceiving self that are implicit in our ontology and epistemology – the self as experienced from the inside, and the self as observed by another self from the outside – a dualism that dogs all of our theories of perception. For a typical example of the kinds of conundrums conventional philosophical thought encounters when addressing these issues see the discussions in Scruton (1998), especially those of self and object, and of persons (chapters 4 and 5). For contrasting explorations from an Eastern perspective, see Loy (1988).
31. Varela, Thompson and Rosch (1991); Noë (2010); Chalmers (1997); McGinn (1999).
32. A nuanced appreciation of this point underlies the approach developed in Varela, Thompson and Rosch (1991).
33. Tallis (1999a). See also Tallis (2012; 2008; 1999b, Chapter 2); Berger (2011a, p. 34).
34. McGinn (1997, p. 64).
35. Candlish and Wrisley (2012); Mulhall (2007); McGinn (2009, Chapter, 4).

5 Ontogenesis and Pathology

1. Winnicott (1964, p. 88).
2. Quoted in Cavalletto (2007, p. 7).
3. Quilley and Loyal (2004, p. 5).
4. Giddens (1992, p. 388).
5. Chalcraft (2007, p. xi).
6. Publisher's product description.
7. Weinstein (2001, p. 91).
8. Platt (1987, p. 221).
9. Elias (1991, pp. 88,18).
10. Hoff (2009), Fàbrega (2001).
11. Sadler (2005, pp. 254–264).
12. The standard psychiatric nosology defined by the American Psychiatric Association (2013) has a near monopoly. There is an interesting, compelling distant competitor and alternative: PDM Task Force (2006). It was assembled by a large group of prominent psychoanalysts and analytically oriented clinical psychologists, but as far as I can see it does not appear to have attracted a significant following outside of the relatively small

number of psychodynamically oriented members of the mental health community.

13. American Psychiatric Association (2013).
14. One of the most interesting and penetrating discussions of this issue that I know is Bartlett (2011). He offers a particularly acute, detailed, sophisticated refutation of equating mental health and the usual conceptions of normality.
15. Sadler.
16. Ryan-Collins, Greenham, Werner and Jackson (2011).
17. Sadler.
18. Sadler.
19. Wittgenstein (1958, p. v).
20. This complex reflexive relationship calls for an approach that is reminiscent of Heidegger's use of the 'hermeneutic circle' – Braver (2007, pp. 164–165).
21. I am greatly oversimplifying the exceedingly complex history of psychoanalysis – see, for example, Turkle (1978). Attitudes toward it differ greatly in different parts of the world.
22. Derrida called it the metaphysics of presence and criticized it at great length. Heidegger called it by many names, including just 'metaphysics'.

23. Berger (especially 1995; also 2009, 2002a and b, 1991, 1985a, 1978). For a comprehensive general analysis of this issue, see Thompson (1981).
24. Piontelli (1992, p. ix).
25. Some support for the hypothesis of genetic memory transmission may be emerging – see Callaway (2013).
26. For example, Grof (2000).
27. For a comprehensive exploration of this 'normal' incoherent splitting of the self, see Olafson (1995). *p. 172*
28. Berger (2005).
29. The qualifier 'as we know it' is intended to alert the reader to the possibility that this way of entering into the language dimension, of hatching, may not be the only option for an infant. I will argue for that possibility in chapters 7 and 8.
30. Harding (2002, p. 68).
31. Harding (1997, p. 16).
32. Bergoffen (1990, p. 222). As I see it, the chief problems with Lacan's view of this process are that he casts it scientistically into incoherent, mystical quasi-mathematical formalisms, and also that he never addresses the problematic nature of the received view of language. The recurrent image of the mirror in many explorations that seek to leave the standard views behind – Heidegger's play of the fourfold, for example – is striking.
33. The physicist Richard Feynman was fond of telling of his father's comment about naming: that you can know the name of a bird in all of the languages of the world, but when you're finished, you'll know absolutely nothing whatever about the bird.
34. Olafson (1995, Chapter 2).
35. Berger (2011a, Chapter 7). Basically, I argue that such paradoxes become possible only under the separability assumption.
36. Dennett (1991); McGilchrist (2009).
37. Berger (2012).
38. Fernyhough (2013); Bermúdez (2003).

39. Candlish and Wrisley (2012); Mulhall (2007); McGinn (2013, pp. 137–138,152, 155–156).
40. Lawson (1985; see also 2001).
41. Braver.
42. This is the initial focus of a host of cognitively oriented developmental studies – see, for example, Ginsburg and Opper (1988); Ingram (1989).
43. Cognitive behaviorists will argue that this is what infants have been doing ever since birth, if not earlier.
44. Braver (2007); Lawson (1985; also 2001).

6   Phylogenesis and Madness

1. The overview of the history of the concept of national character that follows summarizes the discussions in Berger (2009), especially Chapter 2.
2. For some time I have been exploring aspects of cultural pathology in various contexts – see Berger (1991, pp. 53–102; 1985b).
3. Examples are Christopher Lasch's (1979) explorations of narcissism, Eric Fromm's (1955) of the sane society, William Barrett's (1986) of the death of the soul and Kenneth Gergen's (1994) of the mechanical self.
4. Neiburg (2002).
5. Cavalletto (2007, p. 2).
6. Neiburg, Goldman and Gow (2002, p. 69). An example is the construction of the so-called authoritarian personality or f scale that was supposed to identify the pathology underlying Nazism in the Second World War (f stands for fascism).
7. For insightful discussions, see Fromm (1955); Bartlett (2011).
8. Fromm (1955); Kovel (2007); Lasch (1979). Shpard's analysis (1982) is atypical. It emphasizes estrangement from nature, and thus comes closer to the perspective to be developed here.
9. Of course, the hypothesis that our difficulties began with the fall, with the expulsion from paradise of Adam and Eve, draws on an even larger timeframe.
10. Krishnamurti and Bohm (1985, p. 9).
11. Fromm (1955, p. 4).
12. McGilchrist (2009).
13. Sass (1992).
14. See also Tallis (2012 and 2008).
15. Heidegger (1993); Thomson (2005); Lovitt and Lovitt (1995).
16. Wittgenstein (1969–1975, p. 467).
17. Kohn (June 1988); Baumeister and Bushman (2004).
18. Berger (1991); see also Valenstein (1998).
19. It is worth noting that they can do so in some motion pictures and books.
20. Ong (1986, p. 36).
21. Ibid., p. 38. We might recall Freud's warning about the dangers of civilization.
22. Ellis (1993).
23. Barrett (1996, p. xi).

24. Quoted in Owens (1988, p. 52). For an exploration of the commonality in Wittgenstein's and Heidegger's thought, see Braver (2012).
25. Berger (2011a, chapters 6 and 7).
26. However, for a devastating critique of the notion of information, see Tallis (1999a, pp. 88–101).
27. The field now has an extensive literature – see, for example, Baars, Banks and Newman (2003). It even has its own journal.
28. Tallis (1999b, Chapter 2).
29. Ong, p. 24.
30. Braver (2007); I will offer my conception later.
31. Korzybski (1995/1933).
32. Ong (1986, p. 24).
33. Appleyard (2004, p. 120). See also Pauli Pylkkö (1998) for a brilliant analysis of the problems of civilization, presented in the context of Heidegger's Nazism and of civilized rationalism in general.
34. The Pirahã way of life is suggestive in that regard – see Everett (2008).
35. Gore (2008).
36. Berger (2009).
37. I referred to this concept briefly in Chapter 3.
38. See Lewis Wolpert's responses in Goldsmith (2000).
39. Sass (1992).
40. Appleyard (2004); Thomson (2009); Dreyfus (1997, pp. 97–107); Thompson (1981); Hughes (2012).
41. Recent examples are the wildly disproportionate, rabid attacks on Appleyard's (2004) rather tame criticism of scientism.
42. Ong, pp. 24, 29, 32, 43.
43. Braver (2007).
44. The only work I know that takes this approach seriously is Pylkkö (1998).
45. Walsh (2007). In *An Inconvenient Truth*, Al Gore devotes a few short paragraphs to the phenomenon of denial. He illustrates it with a simplistic parable about boiling a frog (2008, pp. 254–255). For an extended and sophisticated critique of Gore's position, see Kovel (2007, Chapter 8). For extended discussions of defensive denial and its treatment, see Berger (2009).
46. Nelson and Timmerman (2011).
47. Ryan-Collins, Greenham, Werner and Jackson (2011); see also Krugman (2012).
48. Watts (1971, Chapter 1).
49. Turkle (2012 and 1984); Greitemeyer and Osswald (2010); Greitemeyer (2014).
50. Berger (2011a, Chapter 7).
51. Winnicott (1965, Chapter 2); Turkle (2012, p. 289).
52. Bartlett (2011).
53. Braver (2007); Armour and Bartlett (1980); Howells (1999, Chapter 1).
54. Berger (2011a, Chapter 7).
55. These have been greatly elucidated in recent scholarship – see Candlish and Wrisley (2012); McGinn (2013).
56. Wittgenstein (1958, §126 and 148).
57. Stolorow and Sanchez (2009).
58. Berger (2012).
59. Wittgenstein (1958, §308).

60. It is the problem that I addressed in my dissertation – Berger (1974), and expanded on for the first time in Berger (1978). At the time I was unaware of Wittgenstein's insightful remarks about states and state processes.

7 Visions of Sanity

1. Bartlett (2011, p. 3).
2. An example of the nefarious but tacit, covert consequences of the received view of language is the assumption that the sentence 'Mental health is . . . ' must have a satisfactory, meaningful completion. The term 'mental health' must have a definable, specifiable referent. That referent must be some something, some existent. But supposing that, like Wittgenstein's 'pain', mental health is neither a something nor a nothing? And supposing, further, that this ascription applies to any and all written squiggles of acoustic bursts, to any concept, word, thought – in fact, that everything in our entire so-called experience, including that experience itself, is neither a something nor a nothing? What then?
3. Shontz (1986, p. 121). The text referred to is Offer and Sabshin (1984).
4. Edwards (1978); Offer and Sabshin.
5. Frances (2010, p. 121).
6. Offer and Sabshin.
7. Bartlett (2014, p. 2).
8. Braver (2012).
9. Owens (1988, p. 66).
10. Owens offers many quotations throughout his paper that support these contentions.
11. Owens.
12. Rorty (1991, p. 52); see also Braver (2012) for discussions of the common elements in these two philosophers' positions.
13. Wittgenstein (1969–75, p. 359). He seems to be pointing to the same kind of duality that Charles Taylor conceptualizes as the difference in children's states before and after their entry into the linguistic dimension (see chapter 3).
14. This material comes from a review of Everett (2008) whose source I have been unable to find.
15. Everett (2008, p. 84).
16. See Colapinto (2007) for similar amusing failed evaluative attempts by Western scientists to evaluate the tribe's cognitive/psychological characteristics. Another important relevant discussion is Charles Taylor's complex philosophical/cross-cultural examination of the notion of rationality, conducted in the context of Peter Winch's analysis of witchcraft among the Azande – Taylor (1985b, chapter 5).
17. I referred to these in Chapter 4 – also Ong (1982, Chapter 3).
18. Everett, p. 179.

8 Toward Restorative Change

1. See especially the discussion of ontotheology in Chapter 1.
2. Ignorance has been defined as knowing a lot of things that aren't so.

3. Appleyard (2004, pp. 139–140).
4. See Appleyard, especially the Preface.
5. Suzuki (1970, pp. 9, 25).
6. Appleyard, p. 9.
7. Appleyard offers exceedingly solid and clear support for his arguments against scientism; see also Goldsmith (2000); H. Smith (2001); B. H. Smith (2005); Dupré (1993); Shepard (1982); Hughes (2012); Tallis(1999a).
8. Appleyard, p. 2.
9. I am not a stranger to this experience.
10. Taylor (1985a, p. 89).
11. A good example in psychiatry is the reductionist blaming of the brain criticized by Valenstein (1998).
12. Turkle (2012).
13. Appleyard, p. xviii.
14. Appleyard; see also the sizable literature stimulated by the 'small is beautiful' approach – Schumacher (1973).
15. Krishnamurti (1960, pp. 12, 13).
16. Berger (2009).
17. Watts (1951, p. 75).
18. Berger (2012). For an intriguing echo, see Watts (1970).
19. Heidegger (1972, p. 2).
20. Summers (2013).
21. Lawson (1985, p. 80).
22. Wynne-Tyson (1985/1988, p. 4). This quotation is the epigraph of Bartlett (2011).
23. Braver (2007).
24. Christopher Lasch's culture of narcissism – see Lasch (1979).
25. Dreikurs (1950).
26. Everett, pp. 55–90.
27. The history of Israel's Kibbutzim may offer some instructive lessons – see Bettelheim (1969).
28. Berger (2009).
29. Bartlett (2011, p. 9).
30. Berger (2009, pp. xii–xiii).
31. Ibid. (2009, p. 89).
32. A recent effort to make this case in psychiatry is Berger (2012).
33. Berger (2011a, pp. 7275, 101, 120).
34. Cited in Braver (2007, p. 21).

References

Abram, David (1997) *The Spell of the Sensuous: Perception and Language in a More-Than-Human World* (New York: Vintage Books).

Aitkenhead, Decca (29 February 2008) 'Enjoy life while you can', *The Guardian*: 33.

American Psychiatric Association (2013) *Diagnostic and Statistical Manual of Mental Disorders*, 5th edition: *DSM-5* (Washington, DC: American Psychiatric Publishing).

Appleyard, Bryan (2004) *Understanding the Present: An Alternative History of Science* (New York: Tauris Parke).

Armour, Leslie and Edward T. Bartlett (1980) *The Conceptualization of the Inner Life* (Atlantic Highlands, NJ: Humanities Press).

Baars, Bernard J., William P. Banks and James B. Newman (eds.) (2003) *Essential Sources in the Scientific Study of Consciousness* (Cambridge: MIT Press).

Barrett, William (1996) 'Introduction', in *Zen Buddhism: Selected Writings of D. T. Suzuki* William Barrett (ed.) (New York: Doubleday).

—— (1986) *Death of the Soul: From Descartes to the Computer* (New York: Anchor Doubleday).

—— (1978) *The Illusion of Technique: A Search for Meaning in a Technological Civilization* (New York: Anchor Press/Doubleday).

Bartlett, Steven J. (2014) 'Afterword', http://www.willamette.edu/~sbartlet/.

—— (2011) *Normality Does Not Equal Mental Health: The Need to Look Elsewhere for Standards of Good Psychological Health* (Santa Barbara, CA: Praeger/Abc-Clio).

Baumann, Gerd (ed.) (1986) *The Written Word* (New York: Oxford University Press).

Baumeister, Roy F. and Brad J. Bushman (2004) 'Human nature and aggressive motivation: Why do cultural animals turn violent?', *Revue Internationale De Psychologie Sociale* 2: 205–220.

Berger, Louis S. (May 2012) 'Confronting psychiatry's occult ontology: A proposal for a new framework', presented at the Twenty-Fourth Annual Meeting of the Association for the Advancement of Philosophy & Psychiatry, Philadelphia.

—— (2011a) *Language and the Ineffable: A Developmental Perspective and Its Applications* (Lanham, MD: Lexington Books).

—— (2011b) Review of John Heaton's *The Talking Cure: Wittgenstein's Therapeutic Method for Psychotherapy*, http://mentalhelp.net/books.

—— (2009) *Averting Global Extinction: Our Irrational Society as Therapy Patient* (Lanham, MD: Jason Aronson).

—— (2005) *The Unboundaried Self: Putting the Person Back Into the View from Nowhere* (Victoria, BC: Trafford).

—— (2002a) *Issues in Psychoanalysis and Psychology: Annotated Collected Papers* (Victoria, BC: Trafford).

—— (2002b) *Psychotherapy as Praxis: Abandoning Misapplied Science* (Victoria, BC: Trafford).

—— (13 May 2000) 'Shortcomings of linguistic/logical models in psychotherapy: An ontological critique', *Tenth Annual Meeting of the Association for the Advancement of Philosophy & Psychiatry*, Chicago.

—— (1995a) 'Grünbaum's questionable interpretations of inanimate systems: "History" and "context" in physics', *Psychoanalytic Psychology* 12: 439–449 (reprinted in Berger, 2002a).

—— (1995b) 'The characteristics and limits of formal representation: Faulconer and Williams's "Temporality in human action" revisited', *Studies in Psychoanalytic Theory* 4: 48–57.

—— (1991) *Substance Abuse as Symptom: A Psychoanalytic Critique of Treatment Approaches and the Cultural Beliefs that Sustain them* (Hillsdale, NJ: Analytic Press).

—— (1985a) *Psychoanalytic Theory and Clinical Relevance: What Makes a Theory Consequential for Practice?* (Hillsdale, NJ: Analytic Press).

—— (1985b, June, August, September, October) 'Notes on depth psychology and peace', Louisville, KY: Council for Peacemaking and Religion Newsletter.

—— (1981) *Introductory Statistics: A New Approach for the Behavioral Sciences* (New York: International Universities Press).

—— (1978) 'Innate constraints of formal theories', *Psychoanalysis and Contemporary Thought* 1: 89–117.

—— (1974) *The Logic of Observation in Psychotherapy Research.* [Unpublished dissertation], University of Tennessee.

—— (1970) 'Barriers to communication between disciplines', *Journal of the Association for the Advancement of Medical Instrumentation* 4: 1.

Bergoffen, Debra B. (1990) 'On Becoming a Subject: Lacan's Rereading of Freud', in *Reconsidering Psychology: Perspectives from Continental Philosophy*, 210–33 edited by James E. Faulconer and Richard N. Williams (Pittsburgh, PA: Duquesne University Press).

Bermúdez, José Luis (2003) *Thinking Without Words* (New York: Oxford University Press).

Bernstein, Richard J. (1992) *The New Constellation* (Cambridge, MA.: MIT Press).

Bettelheim, Bruno (1969) *Children of the Dream: Communal Child-Rearing and American Education* (New York: Macmillan).

Bolton, Derek and Jonathan Hill (2003) *Mind, Meaning, and Mental Disorder: The Nature of Causal Explanation in Psychology and Psychiatry*, 2nd edition (New York: Oxford University Press).

Bouveresse. Jacques (1995) *Wittgenstein Reads Freud: The Myth of the Unconscious*, trans. Carol Cosman (Princeton: Princeton University Press).

Braver, Lee (2012) *Groundless Grounds: A Study of Wittgenstein and Heidegger* (Cambridge: MIT Press).

—— (2007) *A Thing of this World: A History of Continental Anti-Realism* (Evanston: Northwestern University Press).

Cahoone, Lawrence E. (1988) *The Dilemma of Modernity: Philosophy, Culture, and Anti-Culture* (Albany: SUNY Press).

Callaway, Ewen (1 December 2013) 'Fearful memories haunt mouse descendants' http://www.nature.com/.

Candlish, Stewart and George Wrisley (2012) 'Private language', in *The Stanford Encyclopedia of Philosophy*, Edward N. Zalta (ed.). http://plato.stanford.edu.

Carey, Susan (2011) *The Origins of Concepts* (New York: Oxford University Press).

Cavalletto, George (2007) *Crossing the Psycho-social Divide: Freud, Weber, Adorno and Elias* (Burlington, VT: Ashgate Publishing).

Chalcraft, David J. (2007) 'Preface', in *Crossing the Psycho-social Divide: Freud, Weber, Adorno and Elias*, George Cavalletto (Burlington, VT: Ashgate Publishing).

Chalmers, David J. (1997) *The Conscious Mind: In Search of a Fundamental Theory* (New York: Oxford University Press).

Chamberlain, David (1998) *The Mind of Your Newborn Baby* (Berkeley: North Atlantic Books).

Chomsky, Noam and Laray Polk (2013) *Nuclear War and Environmental Catastrophe* (New York: Seven Stories Press).

Colapinto, John (16 April 2007) 'The interpreter', *The New Yorker*: 120–137.

Collins, Harry (2010) *Tacit and Explicit Knowledge* (Chicago: University of Chicago Press).

Dennett, Daniel C. (1991) *Consciousness Explained* (Boston: Little, Brown and Company).

Dreikurs, Rudolf (1950) *Fundamentals of Adlerian Psychology* (New York: Greenberg).

Dreyfus, Hubert L. (1997) 'Heidegger on gaining a free relation to technology', in *Technology and Values* Kristin Shrader-Frecchette and Laura Westra (eds.) (Lanham, MD: Rowman and Littlefield).

Dromm, Keith (2006) 'Wittgenstein on language-learning', *History of Philosophy Quarterly* 23: 79–91.

Dupré, John (1993) *The Disorder of Things: Metaphysical Foundations of the Disunity of Science* (Cambridge: Harvard University Press).

Eagleton, Terry (2003) *After Theory* (New York: Basic Books).

Edwards, J. Guy (1978) 'Normality and abnormality in psychiatry', *British Medical Journal* 2: 1296.

Einstein, Albert (1960) 'The eve of Fascism in Germany', in *Einstein on Peace* Otto Nathan and Heinz Norden (eds.) (New York: Schocken).

Elias, Norbert (1991) *The Society of Individuals*, Michael Schröter (ed.), Edmund Jephcott (trans.) (Cambridge, MA: Basil Blackwell).

Ellis, John M. (1993) *Language, Thought, and Logic* (Evanston: Northwestern University Press).

Everett, Daniel L. (2008) *Don't Sleep, There Are Snakes: Life and Language in the Amazonian Jungle* (New York: Pantheon).

Fàbrega, Horacio Jr. (2001) 'Culture and history in psychiatric diagnosis', *Cultural Psychiatric International Perspectives* 24: 391–405.

Fernyhough, Charles (1 June 2013) 'Life in the Chatter Box', *New Scientist*: 32–35.

Fink, Bruce (1995) *The Lacanian Subject: Between Language and Juissance* (Princeton: Princeton University Press).

Frances, Allen (2010) 'Normality is an endangered species: Psychiatric fads and overdiagnosis', *Psychiatric Times*, http://www.psychiatrictimes.com/.

Freud, Sigmund (1961/1930) *Civilization and its Discontents*, James Strachey (trans.) (New York: Norton).

Fromm, Erich (1955) *The Sane Society* (New York: Holt).

Gergen, Kenneth J. (1994) 'The mechanical self and the rhetoric of objectivity', in *Rethinking Objectivity*, Allan Megill (ed.) (Durham: Duke University Press).

Giddens, Anthony (1992) 'Book review of Norbert Elias's *The Society of Individuals*', *American Journal of Sociology* 98: 388.

Ginsburg, Herbert P. and Sylvia Opper (1988) *Piaget's Theory of Intellectual Development*, 3rd edition (Englewood Cliffs, NJ: Prentice-Hall).

Goldsmith, Edward (May 2000) 'Is science neutral?', *The Ecologist* 30 (pages unavailable)

Goleman, Daniel (27 August 1992) 'Study finds babies at 5 months grasp simple mathematics', *New York Times*.

Gore, Al (2008) *An Inconvenient Truth: The Planetary Emergency of Global Warming and What We Can Do about It* (New York: Rodale).

Gottlieb, Anthony (2000) *The Dream of Reason: A History of Philosophy from the Greeks to the Renaissance* (New York: Norton).

Gray, Paul (1994) *The Ego and Analysis of Defense* (Northvale, NJ: Jason Aronson).

Greitemeyer, Tobias (2014) 'Playing violent video games increases intergroup bias', *Personality and Social Psychology Bulletin* 40: 70–78.

——, and Silvia Osswald (2010) 'The effects of prosocial video games on prosocial conduct', *Journal of Personality and Social Psychology* 98: 211–221.

Grof, Stanislav (2000) *Psychology of the Future: Lessons from Modern Consciousness Research* (Albany: SUNY Press).

—— (1985) *Beyond the Brain: Birth, Death and Transcendence in Psychotherapy* (Albany, N.Y.: State University of New York Press).

Guignon, Charles B. (1983) *Heidegger and the Problem of Knowledge* (Indianapolis, IN.: Hackett).

Harris, Roy (2005) *The Semantics of Science* (London: Continuum).

—— (2000) *Rethinking Writing* (Bloomington: Indiana University Press).

—— (1996) *The Language Connection: Philosophy and Linguistics* (Dulles, VA.: Thoemmes Press).

—— (1990) *The Foundations of Linguistic Theory: Selected Writings of Roy Harris* Nigel Love (ed.) (New York: Routledge).

Havelock, Eric A. (1986) *The Muse Learns to Write: Reflections on Orality and Literacy from Antiquity to the Present* (New Haven, CT: Yale University Press).

Heidegger, Martin (1996) *The Principle of Reason*, trans. Reginald Lilly (Bloomington: Indiana University Press).

—— (1996/1927) *Being and Time*, trans. Joan Stambaugh (Albany: SUNY Press).

—— (1993) 'The question concerning technology', in *Basic Writings*, David Krell (ed.) (New York: HarperCollins).

—— (1972) *On Time and Being*, trans. Joan Stambaugh (New York: Harper Torchbooks).

Hinshaw, Virgil G., Jr., 'Einstein's social philosophy', in *Albert Einstein, Philosopher-Scientist* Paul A. Schilpp (ed.) (New York: MJF Books).

Hoff, Paul (2009) 'Historical roots of the concept of mental illness' in *Psychiatric Diagnosis: Challenges and Prospects*, Ihsan M. Salloum and Juan E. Mezzich (eds.). (New York: Wiley).

Howells, Christina (1999) *Derrida: Deconstruction from Phenomenology to Ethics* (Malden, MA: Blackwell).

Ingram, David (1989) *First Language Acquisition: Method, Description and Explanation* (New York: Cambridge University Press).

Kohn, Alfie (June 1988) 'Are humans innately aggressive?', *Psychology Today*: 35–38.

Korzybski, Alfred (1995/1933) *Science and Sanity: An Introduction to Non-Aristotelian Systems and General Semantics* (Englewood, NJ: Institute of General Semantics).

Kovel, Joel (2007) *The Enemy of Nature: The End of Capitalism or the End of the World?* 2nd edition (New York: Zed Books).

Krishnamurti, Jiddu (1960) *Commentaries on Living: 3rd Series* (New York: Harper)

——, and David Bohm (1985) *The Ending of Time* (San Francisco: HarperSanFrancisco).

Krugman, Paul (2 January 2012) 'Nobody understands debt', *New York Times*, A12.

Kuhl, Patricia K. (2000) 'A new view of language acquisition', *Proceedings of the National Academy of Sciences of the United States of America* 97: 11850–11857.

Kusch, Martin (1995) *Psychologism: A Case Study in the Sociology of Philosophical Knowledge* (New York: Routledge).

Lafont, Cristina (2000) *Heidegger, Language, and World-Disclosure*, trans. Graham Harman (New York: Cambridge University Press).

Lakoff, George and Rafael E. Núñez (2000) *Where Mathematics Comes From: How the Embodied Mind Brings Mathematics into Being* (New York: Basic Books).

Laplace, Pierre Simon (1902) *A Philosophical Essay on Probabilities* (New York: Wiley).

Lasch, Christopher (1979) *The Culture of Narcissism: American Life in an Age of Diminishing Expectations* (New York: Norton).

Lawson, Hilary (2001) *Closure: A Story of Everything* (New York: Routledge).

—— (1985) *Reflexivity: The Post-Modern Predicament* (La Salle, IL: Open Court).

Loewald, Hans (1980) *Papers on Psychoanalysis* (New Haven: Yale University Press).

Lovitt, William and Harriet Brundage Lovitt (1995) *Modern Technology in the Heideggerian Perspective*, 2 vols. (Lewiston, New York: Edwin Mellen Press).

Loy, David (1988) *Nonduality: A Study in Comparative Philosophy* (New Haven: Yale University Press).

Macnamara, John (1999) *Through the Rearview Mirror: Historical Reflections on Psychology* (Cambridge: MIT Press).

McGilchrist, Iain (2009) *The Master and his Emissary: The Divided Brain and the Making of the Western World* (New Haven, CT: Yale University Press).

McGinn, Colin (1999) *The Mysterious Flame: Conscious Minds in a Material World* (New York: Basic Books).

—— (1997) *The Character of Mind: An Introduction to the Philosophy of Mind* (New York: Oxford University Press).

McGinn, Marie (2013) *Routledge Guidebook to Wittgenstein's Philosophical Investigations* (New York: Routledge, 2013).

—— (2009) *Elucidating the* Tractatus: *Wittgenstein's Early Philosophy of Logic and Language* (New York: Oxford University Press).

Mahler, Margaret S., Fred Pine, and Anni Bergman (1975) *The Psychological Birth of the Human Infant: Symbiosis and Individuation* (New York: Basic Books).

Monk, Ray (2005) *How to Read Wittgenstein* (New York: Norton).

Mulhall, Stephen (2007) *Wittgenstein's Private Language: Grammar, Nonsense and Imagination in Philosophical Investigations*, §§243–315 (New York: Oxford University Press).

Nagel, Thomas (1986) *The View from Nowhere* (New York: Oxford University Press).

—— (1974) 'What is it like to be a bat?', *Philosophical Review* 83: 435–450.

Neiburg, Federico (2002) 'National character', https://webspace.yale.edu/.

——, Marcio Goldman and Peter Gow (2002) 'Anthropology and politics in studies of national character', *Cultural Anthropology* 13: 56–81.

Nelson, Anitra and Frans Timmerman (eds.) (2011) *Life Without Money: Building Fair and Sustainable Economies* (London: Pluto Press).

Noë, Alva (2010) *Out of Our Heads: Why You Are Not Your Brain, and Other Lessons from the Biology of Consciousness* (New York: Hill and Wang).

Nugent, J. Kevin (2013) 'The competent newborn and the neonatal behavioral assessment scale: T. Berry Brazelton's legacy', *Journal of Child and Adolescent Psychiatric Nursing* 26: 173–179.

—— and Abelardo Morell (2011) *Your Baby Is Speaking to You: A Visual Guide to the Amazing Behaviors of Your Newborn and Growing Baby* (New York: Houghton Mifflin Harcourt).

Offer, Daniel and Melvin Sabshin (eds.) (1984) *Normality and the Life Cycle: A Critical Integration* (New York: Basic Books).

Olafson, Frederick A. (1995) *What is a Human Being? A Heideggerian View* (New York: Cambridge University Press).

Olson, David R. (2006) 'Oral discourse in a world of literacy', *Research in the Teaching of English* 41: 136–143.

—— (1994) *The World on Paper: The Conceptual and Cognitive Implications of Writing and Reading* (New York: Cambridge University Press).

Ong, Walter (1988) 'Before textuality: Orality and interpretation', *Oral Tradition* 3: 259–269.

—— (1986) 'Writing is a technology that restructures thought', in *The Written Word* (ed.) Gerd Baumann. (New York: Oxford University Press).

—— (1982) *Orality and Literacy: The Technologizing of the Word* (New York: Methuen).

Owens, Wayne D. (1988) 'Heidegger and the philosophy of language', *Auslegung* 14: 50–66.

PDM Task Force (2006) *Psychodynamic Diagnostic Manual* (Silver Springs, MD: Alliance of Psychoanalytic Organizations).

Piontelli, Alessandra (1992) 'Editor's preface', in *From Fetus to Child: An Observational and Psychoanalytic Study* (New York: Routledge).

Platt, Gerald M. (1987) 'The psychoanalytic sociology of collective behavior: Material interests, cultural factors, and emotional responses in revolution', in *Advances in Psychoanalytic Sociology* Jerome Rabow, Gerald M. Platt and Marion S. Goldman (eds.) (Malabar, FL: Robert E. Krieger).

Prado, C. G. (1992) *Descartes and Foucault: A Contrastive Introduction to Philosophy* (Ottawa, Can.: University of Ottawa Press).

Pylkkö, Pauli (1998) *The Aconceptual Mind: Heideggerian Themes in Holistic Naturalism* (Philadelphia: Benjamin).

Quilley, Stephen and Steven Loyal (2004) 'Towards a "central theory": The scope and relevance of the sociology of Norbert Elias', in *The Sociology of Norbert Elias* Steven Loyal and Stephen Quilley (eds.) (New York: Cambridge University Press).

Quine, W. V. O. (1960) *Word and Object* (Cambridge: MIT Press).

Robinson, Ian (1975) *The New Grammarians' Funeral: A Critique of Noam Chomsky's Linguistics* (New York: Cambridge University Press).

Romanos, George D. (1983) *Quine and Analytic Philosophy: The Language of Language* (Cambridge, MA: MIT Press).

Rorty, Richard (1991) *Essays on Heidegger and Others: Philosophical Papers*, vol. 2 (New York: Cambridge University Press).

Ryan-Collins, Josh, Tony Greenham, Richard Werner and Andrew Jackson (2011) *Where Does Money Come From?* (London: New Economics Foundation).

Sadler, John Z. (2005) *Values and Psychiatric Diagnosis* (New York: Oxford University Press).

Sass, Louis (1992) *Madness and Modernism: Insanity in the Light of Modern Art, Literature, and Thought* (New York: Basic Books).

Schumacher, E. F. A. (1973) *Small Is Beautiful: Economics as If People Mattered* (New York: Harper & Row).

Scribner, Sylvia and Michael Cole (1981) *The Psychology of Literacy* (Cambridge: Harvard University Press).

Scruton, Roger (1998) *An Intelligent Person's Guide to Philosophy* (New York: Penguin Putnam).

Segal, Hanna (1995) 'From Hiroshima to the Gulf war and after: A psychoanalytic perspective', in *Psychoanalysis in Contexts: Paths Between Theory and Modern Culture*, Anthony Elliott and Stephen Frosh (eds.) (New York: Routledge).

Shepard, Paul (1982) *Nature and Madness* (Athens, GA: University of Georgia Press).

Sheldrake, Rupert (2003) *The Sense of Being Stared At: And Other Unexplained Powers of the Human Mind.* (New York: Crown).

Shontz, Franklin C. (1986) 'Review of normality and the life cycle: A critical integration', *Rehabilitation Psychology* 31: 121–123.

Smith, Barbara Herrnstein (2005) *Scandalous Knowledge: Science, Truth and the Human* (Durham: Duke University Press).

Smith, Huston (2001) *Why Religion Matters: The Fate of the Human Spirit in an Age of Disbelief* (San Francisco: HarperSanFrancisco).

Soukup, Paul A., S. J. (2013) 'Book review: A hundred years of Walter Ong', *Center for the Study of Communication and Culture* 26: 3–33.

Stolorow, Robert D. and Robert Eli Sanchez (2009) 'Philosophy as therapy: The case of Heidegger', *International Journal of Psychoanalytic Self Psychology* 1: 125–131.

Summers, Frank (25 April 2013) 'Psychoanalysis in the Age of Nikeism', Presidential Address, Annual Spring Conference, Division of Psychoanalysis, *American Psychological Association*. Available at http://www.psychologytoday.com/blog/meaningful-you/201305/psychoanalysis-in-the-age-just-do-it.

Suzuki, Daisetz Teitaro (1970) 'Lectures on Buddhism', in *Zen Buddhism and Psychoanalysis* Erich Fromm, D. T. Suzuki and Richard DeMartino (eds.) (New York: Harper & Row).

Tallis, Raymond (2012) *Aping Mankind: Neuromania, Darwinitis and the Misrepresentation of Humanity* (Durham: Acumen).

—— (2008) *The Kingdom of Infinite Space: A Portrait of Your Head* (New Haven: Yale University Press).

—— (1999a) *The Explicit Animal: A Defence of Human Consciousness*, reprint of the 1991 (ed.) with a new preface (New York: St. Martin's Press).

—— (1999b) *On the Edge of Certainty: Philosophical Explorations* (New York: St. Martin's Press).

Taylor, Charles (1995) *Philosophical Arguments* (Cambridge: Harvard University Press).

—— (1985a) *Human Agency and Language: Philosophical Papers 1* (New York: Cambridge University Press).

—— (1985b) *Philosophy and the Human Sciences: Philosophical Papers 2* (New York: Cambridge University Press).

Thompson, Richard L. (1981) *Mechanistic and Nonmechanistic Science: An Investigation into the Nature of Consciousness and Form* (Lynbrook, N.Y.: Bala Books).

Thomson, Iain (2009) 'Understanding technology Ontotheologically, or: Danger and the promise of Heidegger, an American perspective', in *New Waves in the Philosophy of Technology,* Jan-Kyrre Berg Olsen, Evan Selinger and Soren Riis (eds.) (New York: Palgrave Macmillan).

—— (2005) *Heidegger on Ontotheology: Technology and the Politics of Education* (New York: Cambridge University Press).

Turkle, Sherry (2012) *Alone Together: Why We Expect More from Technology and Less from Each Other* (New York: Basic Books).

—— (1984) *The Second Self: Computers and the Human Spirit* (New York: Simon and Schuster).

—— (1978) *Psychoanalytic Politics: Freud's French Revolution* (New York: Basic Books).

Valenstein, Elliot S. (1998) *Blaming the Brain: About Drugs and Mental Health* (New York: Free Press).

Varela, Francisco, Evan Thompson, and Eleanor Rosch (1991) *The Embodied Mind* (Cambridge, MA: MIT Press).

Wakeley, Ann, Susan Rivera and Jonas Langer (2000) 'Can young children add and subtract?', *Child Development* 71: 1525–1534.

Walsh, Bryan (2007) 'Q & A: Talking to Al Gore', *Time,* http://www.time.com/time/specials/2007/personoftheyear/.

Watts, Alan W. (1971) *Does it Matter? Essays on Man's Relation to Materiality* (New York: Vintage Books).

—— (1970) 'What's wrong with the world?', http://www.youtube.com/watch?v=_LXiSPpfM54.

—— (1951) *The Wisdom of Insecurity* (New York: Pantheon).

Weinstein, Fred (2001) *Freud, Psychoanalysis, Social Theory: The Unfulfilled Promise* (Albany: SUNY Press).

Winnicott, Donald (1965) *The Maturational Processes and the Facilitating Environment* (New York: International Universities Press).

—— (1964/1947) 'Further thoughts on babies as persons', in *The Child, the Family, and the Outside World* (Harmondsworth, GB: Penguin Books).

Wittgenstein, Ludwig (1958)*Philosophical Investigations,* 3rd edition and trans. G. E. M. Anscombe (New York: Macmillan).

—— (1969–1975) *On Certainty,* trans. Denis Paul and G. E. M. Anscombe (Oxford: Basil Blackwell).

Wynne-Tyson, Jon (1985/1988) *The Extended Circle: Dictionary of Humane Thought* (Jackson, TN: Marlowe).

Young, Julian (2002) *Heidegger's Later Philosophy* (New York: Cambridge University Press).

Index

Note: The letter 'n' following locators refers to notes.

CPSIA information can be obtained at www.ICGtesting.com
Printed in the USA
BVOW08*0113300315

393781BV00007B/31/P